Advancing a Different Modernism

T0386335

Advancing a Different Modernism analyzes a long-ignored but formative aspect of modern architecture and art. By examining selective buildings by the Catalan architect Lluís Domènech i Montaner (1850–1923) and by the Slovenian designer Jože Plecnik (1872–1957), the book reveals the fundamental political and ideological conservatism that helped shape modernism's history and purpose. This study thus revises the dominant view of modernism as a union of progressive forms and progressive politics. Instead, this innovative volume promotes a nuanced and critical consideration of how architecture was creatively employed to advance radically new forms and methods, while simultaneously consolidating an essentially conservative nationalist self-image.

Steven Mansbach is Distinguished University Professor and Professor of the History of Twentieth-Century Art at the University of Maryland

"With *Advancing a Different Modernism*, Mansbach, already recognized as one of the pre-eminent scholars of Central European modernism, moves the field in an exciting and stimulating direction, looking beyond the 'classics' of modernism and incorporating works of artists for whom the ideas and ideals of nationalism, and its role in modernism, were profoundly formative."

– Samuel D. Albert, Fashion Institute of Technology

Routledge Focus on Art History and Visual Studies

1 **Advancing a Different Modernism**
S. A. Mansbach

Advancing a Different Modernism

S.A. Mansbach

Routledge
Taylor & Francis Group

LONDON AND NEW YORK

First published 2018 by Routledge

2 Park Square, Milton Park, Abingdon, Oxon OX14 4RN

605 Third Avenue, New York, NY 10017

Routledge is an imprint of the Taylor & Francis Group, an informa business

First issued in paperback 2021

Publisher's Note

The publisher has gone to great lengths to ensure the quality of this reprint but points out that some imperfections in the original copies may be apparent.

Library of Congress Cataloging in Publication Data
A catalog record for this book has been requested

ISBN: 978-1-138-57493-9 (hbk)
ISBN: 978-1-03-217888-2 (pbk)
DOI: 10.4324/9781351273008

Typeset in Times New Roman
by codeMantra

Contents

Illustration List

Acknowledgements

The modest size of the present volume is belied by the magnitude of assistance and expertise that has been contributed by colleagues and friends. All merit recognition and the author's abiding gratitude.

Professor José María Naharrro-Calderón and art historian Àngels Ferret-Ballester were selfless and creative in providing the first full English translation of Domènech i Montaner's essential "En Busca de la Arquitectura nacional", so critical to the development of modern art and the national spirit of Catalonia. The translation constitutes the book's appendix.

In Barcelona I had the privilege of working with Professor Antoni Bover Tanyà and Miquel Bigas Tañà of the Universitat Politècnica de Catalunya (CITM) and La Farinera, Centre d'Arts Visuals de Vic. In addition, Antoni, Miquel, and I were granted special permission to study and photograph the Palau de la Música Catalana, the Hospital de la Santa Creu i Sant Pau, and the Casa de les Punxes through the gracious hospitality of Núria Queralt, Mercè Beltrand, and Montse Jimènez, respectively.

For decades I have benefitted from the knowledge and friendship of Damjan Prelovšek, with whom I first taught in Prague in the early 1990s and through whose guidance I have been taken to a host of Plečnik monuments throughout Central Europe ever since. His work on the Slovene architect remains the standard for historical scholarship on Plečnik, his Central European contemporaries, and his period.

I am also grateful to Dr. Andrej Smrekar in Ljubljana, who has been an ideal travel companion with whom to visit Plečnik's buildings and to see the work of so many of the Slovene's confederates' endeavors, the better to establish a rich architectural context. I am especially indebted to Dr. Peter Zacherl for the time he devoted to taking Andrej Smrekar and me on an intensive tour of the Zacherlhaus in Vienna, which his grandfather commissioned and whose architectural integrity Peter safeguards.

The present volume has been enriched, as have my much longer scholarly studies treating aspects Central European visual culture, by the stimulating conversation, creative exchange of ideas, and unstinting encouragement of Professor Anthony Alofsin. For his companionship over so many years, I am grateful.

Dr. Therese O'Malley, Associate Dean of the Center for Advanced Study in the Visual Arts at the National Gallery of Art, Washington, was the co-originator of the conference devoted to "Modernism and Landscape Architecture, 1890–1940" in which I first presented some of my ideas regarding Plečnik's landscape architecture. The resulting volume of the same title (2015) contains material that is represented in a different context in Chapter 3. I thank her and the Trustees of the National Gallery of Art for their support.

To Dr. Henry Duval Gregory I am deeply indebted for his extraordinary range of expertise regarding how best to treat sensitively images and texts. His combination of scholarship and digital mastery is a model one wishes one could emulate.

My wife Julia has not only been a loving critic, but has long proven to be an excellent and tolerant traveling partner, as well as an essential photographer. I can only hope my gratitude expressed here might burnish the inherent pleasures of being together in Catalonia and Slovenia, as well as in Vienna.

1   Critical and Theoretical Introduction

For decades, sensitive readers of modernism have recognized its variability, contingency, and specificity.[1] Although there are general stylistic affinities within modernism, the specific sources of these formal characteristics often refer to indigenous traditions or forms, to shared historical references such as a stripped-down classicism or neo-classicism or even to religious or quasi-religious doctrine ranging from Calvinism to anthroposophy. Despite the productive practice of noting the complexities and not infrequent contradictions within modernist visual expression, cultural historians are apparently less prepared to grant a similar variableness when it comes to the political or ideological motivations (or desired consequences) of modernism.[2] Here, it seems as if a kind of historiographical inertia is at work, one that persists in equating modernism and political progressivism, or advanced art (of most any style) and liberal social formation.[3] It is important to stress here that I am not impugning the fundamentally redemptive character that lay at the creative core of modernist aesthetics generally.[4] Rather, I wish only to urge a more nuanced and critical consideration of how modernism has been prompted by and periodically achieved an "alternative success" by affirming a conservative valence. This is not to argue for the advantage of one politics over another, or to assign modern art to a conservative camp or a liberal democratic world view. Instead, the present argument affirms the essential multiplicity of a historical modernizing art and architecture and recognizes how it was elaborated to advance a less well-acknowledged set of social aspirations. In the end, studies of the kind conducted here will restore to modern art its inherent complexity and multivalence, a diversity that has been long suppressed by the practice, prejudices, and programs of two generations of historians, critics, and artists themselves.

As many scholars have demonstrated, the rise of nationalist movements during the 19th century frequently resulted in contention between inherently conservative political groups and broadly liberal ones in which cultural identity was a principal battleground.[5] In much of Europe, nationalism was invoked with equal passion on a more narrowly focused engagement with a cultural, ethnic, or "racial" sub-nationalism, which did, of course, frequently mirror the ideological contentiousness of large-scale, nation-state nationalism. Thus, for instance, a Breton "national revival" was underway at the same time an ardent struggle over an authentic "French" identity was waged, especially in the years following the 1870 French humiliation at Sedan.[6] Similar struggles between "greater" and "narrower" nationalisms were waged in Norway during Swedish suzerainty, in the Baltic lands inhabited by Estonians and Latvians under the scepter of the Tsar, in partitioned Poland, and perhaps most pronouncedly in the multiethnic, multi-confessional lands subject to the Dual Monarchy of Austria-Hungary. All embraced the arts as an effective means by which to redeem a suppressed, lost, or imagined identity in the face of a dominant "national" or international power.[7]

Although folk motives were a favored emblem of "locality" almost universally,[8] their forms, colors, and abstract patterns were not infrequently represented or referenced in rigorously modern idioms through which the "national" character could be demonstrated to be simultaneously ethnically distinctive and thoroughly contemporary. By invoking nativist patterns and re-presenting their abstract forms, a conservative historical reference was coupled with a modernist (and transnational) expressiveness. Such practice, rooted in 19th-century European historicism continued into the high modernism decade of the 1920s, as a Latvian plate well illustrates. Here, for instance, Romans Suta (1896–1944) creatively combines native, pre-Slavic and pre-Teutonic references to Ur-Baltic tribal imagery with the Spartan geometry of Suprematist forms that populate the rim (Figure 1.1).

Although Suta's porcelain designs reconcile a backward-looking Latvian nativism with a formal revolutionary utopianism,[9] such inventive ideological and artistic "blends" were less oxymoronic than symptomatic of a common practice all too often overlooked by contemporary commentators.

Too little attention has been paid to this creative combination of conservative reference and ideology on the one hand, and modernist methods and forms on the other, due to a prevailing association of liberal values with modernist forms. Although powerfully advanced by many of modernism's greatest innovators through persuasive

Figure 1.1 Romans Suta, *Wedding*, "Baltars" porcelain plate, ca. 1926.
Source: Photo courtesy of the Latvian National Museum of Art's Department of Decorative Arts and Design, Riga.

publications – journals, books, and manifestoes – and innovatively institutionalized through revolutionary academies (from the German Bauhaus to the Russian Vkhutemas), the union of liberal attitudes and revolutionary forms represents only one side of fully rounded modernism. Indeed, scholars have pointed out that even the most respected of the modernist figures, such as Walter Gropius and Ludwig Mies van der Rohe, sought to accommodate their daring pedagogical and architectural programs to the demands both of leftist local governments and, later, to the (early) Nazi regime.[10] A similar ideological flexibility can be observed through much of Europe during the first third of the 20th century, when modernists negotiated between democracy and dictatorship, a reactionary nativism and a liberal transnationalism.

This ideological multifariousness had its historical impetus in the late 19th and early 20th centuries, a time when comparative studies often brought to the surface art's variability, both stylistically and conceptually. However, this once dominant mode of discourse has long been discredited, as it was nefariously employed under authoritarian regimes to promote claims of ethnic, national, or racial priority.[11] Nonetheless, the self-awareness and open-mindedness that characterize poststructuralist study of modernism encourage a reconsideration of the conservative valence of modernist aesthetics. To do so is to recognize that there is a salutary complement to the liberal (or radical) aspect of avant-garde aesthetics, and that *together* the wholeness of modernism might best be perceived.

Perhaps no two examples more instructively represent a creative conservative amalgam of aesthetic progressivism and ideology than the Catalonian *modernisme* of Lluís Domènech i Montaner (1850–1923) and his circle,[12] and the idiosyncratic modernism of the Slovenian architect, planner, and designer, Jože Plečnik (1872–1957).[13] Each pursued an ingenious expression appropriate for a modernizing era; and each acknowledged the gravitational pull of local history, traditions, and religious values, even if the architects' conceptions of them were more aspirational than factual.

Although the arenas where Domènech and Plečnik were most active might today seem geographically marginal, one must keep in mind that Barcelona, Vienna, and Ljubljana (then known primarily under its German name of Laibach) were sites of stunning cultural creativity from the late 19th century through the early decades of the 20th century. Perhaps, some of the creative ferment was even fostered by the cities' distance from the strong gravitational magnetism exerted by Paris, Munich, Milan, and Berlin, which are customarily cited by historians as primary creative capitals. Indeed, being on the "periphery" often permitted the very experimentation and the inventive adaptation of artistic forms and purposes that frequently were constrained by the tempo, expectations, and markets in such a long-established cosmopolitan capital as Paris. Of course, Vienna surely occupied the first rank of world artistic centers, even if its legion of artists, intellectuals, and industrialist patrons promoted forms of cultural rebellion against Habsburg conservatism and its formal institutions to a degree that was likely unequalled elsewhere.[14] And thus, it was not anomalous that Plečnik, a provincial from Slovenia, would be able to make his mark on the imperial capital just a stone's throw from its revered medieval cathedral, just as other aspiring artists endeavored to create revolutionary work in the various capitals of the Habsburg realm: Lemberg, Prague, and, especially during this era, Budapest.[15]

Plečnik was peripatetic, moving among Vienna, Prague, and Laibach, where in each context he creatively melded innovative aesthetics with an often idiosyncratic political and social reactionarism. By working with established architects and designers in Vienna; by collaborating with Tomáš Garrigue Masaryk, the first president of Czechoslovakia, in Prague; and by accepting a series of commissions from the city fathers of his native city, Plečnik sought to demonstrate the richness of his architectural (and design) vision for modern humankind while consolidating a visual idiom particular to a Slavic people. Domènech, by contrast, confined his activities, both architectural and governmental, principally to Barcelona and Catalonia, where his creative work as an architect, theoretician, and politician was predicated on developing and implementing a distinctive Catalan expression, one through which native elements could be reconfigured into a modernist idiom appropriate for a modernizing, self-aware "nation."

By choosing these two figures as a principal focus of this study, I do not wish to dismiss the legion of other modernists who seized upon progressive aesthetics to promote a conservative, often reactionary or ultramontane cultural-political ideology. Rather, it is important to acknowledge that Plečnik and Domènech may offer the historian the ideal (and idealistic) exemplars of an alternative modernism that has rarely been incorporated in studies of the history of modern – viz., progressive – art and architecture. As is argued in the following pages, each architect created seminal monuments of advanced architecture, while combining them – and often justifying them – with a forceful advocacy of political conservatism. This heady blend of innovative styles and forward-thinking methods was combined with a rejection of the kinds of liberalism we are accustomed to expect from reformist artists. This having been said, it is not the necessary revision of our present-day expectations that attending to the modernism of Plečnik and Domènech fosters. Rather, a consideration of the work and inspiration of Plečnik and Domènech encourages us to accept the inherent complexity and contradiction of the modernist enterprise itself.

The following chapters can be read independently; however, each is enriched when considered in the context of the other. For though the geographical contexts and historical traditions differ greatly between the Barcelona of Domènech and the Habsburg Vienna and Yugoslav Ljubljana of Plečnik, each architect responded inventively and in a notably parallel manner to the challenges of creating a modernism fit for a people eager to consolidate its distinctive nationhood.

Finally, this volume contains an appendix. Although the desired symmetry of this study would have been furthered by including an important original document (and translation into English) by both

Plečnik and Domènech, Plečnik, unlike Domènech, was less inclined to be explicitly theoretical. Hence, he published few pivotal texts; moreover, many of his letters communicating his thoughts and registering his reflections have already been published (mostly in the languages he was able to write fluently: principally German, Czech, and Slovenian; and translated in the English-language texts as cited in the endnotes below). By contrast, Domènech was consistently engaged in articulating an architectural program of nationalistic purpose and application. As a result, his writings help to explain his architecture, just as his architecture might be comprehended as the material realization of his published political positions. Because of the centrality of his writings to his art, and in light of the seminal influence his published articles have exerted on generations of Catalonians, presenting Domènech's principal essay for the first time in English is both appropriate for a fuller appreciation of the architect's objectives as well as fitting for an understanding of *modernisme*'s continuing influence.

Notes

1   In the last 20 years or so, a number of studies have promoted a helpful perspective through which to reassess the meanings and purposes of modernist architecture. Many of those treating "national" histories of modern architecture have appeared under the rubric of Docomomo (International Working Party for Documentation and Conservation of Buildings, Sites and Neighbourhoods of the Modern Movement). Most are premised on the concept of a pluralistic modernism; that is, a methodological strategy that holds that progressive architectural forms and uses defy any unitary categorical imperative. In contrast to the dominant interpretive uniformity that characterized the plurality of architectural studies from the 1930s into the 1990s, they attribute to modernism a heterogeneity of meanings and intentions. Representative of the current historiographical orientation are Hubert-Jan Henckert and Hilde Heynen, eds., *Back from Utopia: The Challenge of the Modern Movement* (Rotterdam: 010 Publishers, 2002); Hilde Heynen, *Architecture and Modernity: A Critique* (Cambridge, MA: The MIT Press, 1999); and *Universality and Heterogeneity, Proceedings from the Fourth International Docomomo Conference* (18–21 September 1996) (Bratislava, 1997). See also, S. A. Mansbach, "Modernist Architecture and Nationalist Aspiration in the Baltic: Two Case Studies," *Journal of the Society of Architectural Historians*, vol. 65, no. 1, March 2006, pp. 92–111.
2   See Jeffrey Herf, *Reactionary Modernism: Technology, Culture, and Politics in Weimar and the Third Reich* (Cambridge: Cambridge University Press, 1984), and Kathleen James-Chakraborty, ed., *Bauhaus Culture from Weimar to the Cold War* (Minneapolis: University of Minnesota Press, 2006).
3   One might cite as a telling example, the two-volume survey of 20th-century art by Hal Foster, Rosalind Krauss, Yve-Alain Bois, Benjamin H. D. Buchloh, and David Joselit, *Art Since 1900: Modernism Antimodernism*

Postmodernism (London: Thames & Hudson, 2005). More narrowly focused and historically justified in this context is the work of Patricia Leighten and Mark Antliff, especially Leighten's *The Liberation of Painting: Modernism and Anarchism in Avant-Guerre Paris* (Chicago, IL: University of Chicago Press, 2013) and *Re-Ordering the Universe: Picasso and Anarchism, 1897–1914* (Princeton, NJ: Princeton University Press, 1989); and Antliff's *Avant-Garde Fascism: The Mobilization of Myth, Art and Culture in France, 1909–1939* (Durham, NC: Duke University Press, 2007) as well as *Fascist Visions: Art and Ideology in France and Italy* (with Matthew Affron, Princeton, NJ: Princeton University Press, 1997), and *Cubism and Culture* (with Patricia Leighten, London: Thames and Hudson, 2001). A traditional viewpoint, well-documented and cogently argued, has been advanced by Neil McWilliam and informs his searching current study on *The Aesthetics of Reaction*, which he describes an investigation into

> ...the complex relationship between nationalism, traditionalism and the critique of modern culture in France.... Coinciding with the explosive challenge to established forms and subject matter in the visual arts promoted by avant-garde circles in Paris, conservatives attempted to reassert values ostensibly rooted in the character and cultural genealogy of the French nation. This anti-modernist reaction was promoted by nationalist critics and political theorists who sought to salvage French culture as part of a broader project that challenged liberal democratic institutions.

4   As early as the 1970s I have been arguing for the fundamentally redemptive aspiration that informed abstract art, especially the geometrical abstraction developed by and justified through the writings of Theo van Doesburg, Laszlo Moholy-Nagy, El Lissitzky, and many others. See Mansbach, *Visions of Totality: Theo van Doesburg, Laszlo Moholy-Nagy, and El Lissitzky* (Ann Arbor, MI: Research Press, 1979).

5   See Richard Etlin, ed., *Nationalism in the Visual Arts (Studies in the History of Art)* (Washington, DC: National Gallery of Art; Distributed by the University Press of New England, 1991); Françoise Forster-Hahn, ed., *Imagining Modern German Culture, 1889–1910 (Studies in the History of Art)* (Washington, DC: National Gallery of Art; Distributed by the University Press of New England, 1996); and June Hargrove and Neil McWilliam, eds., *Nationalism and French Visual Culture, 1870–1914 (Studies in the History of Art)* (Washington, DC: National Gallery of Art; Distributed by Yale University Press, 2005).

6   With the defeat of the French by German armies, the Deutsches Reich was consolidated, which, somewhat paradoxically, allowed for many of its constituent states and statelets to continue to manifest their respective traditions without fear of undermining German unity (excluding, of course, the Habsburg lands, which remained independent of Berlin).

7   In these, and most other instances, local nationalisms were divided less explicitly by politics or class than motivated by linguistic, religious, or cultural affiliations.

8   This was evident in almost all the arts: plastic, musical, and literary. Indeed, one could argue that (sub)National Romanticism was itself an ideated "localism" enlarged by the desire for a potent "ethnic" identity. See, for example, the special issue of *Centropa* (vol. 2, no. 1, January 2002) devoted to National Romanticism.

9   The geometrical abstraction evident on the plate's rim can be recognized as the artist's acknowledgment of the revolutionary use of Constructivist and Supramatist forms by Ilya Chasnik and Nikolai Suetin, and of course by their teacher Kazimir Malevich, in adjacent Bolshevist Russia. Suta would have known the Bolshevist artists' abstract canvases as well as their propaganda porcelain that embraced these geometrical forms from the former's study of both published reproductions and actual pieces that circulated in the Latvian Republic despite official opposition to the Russian regime. Further, Suta would have been familiar with this mode of modernism through his persistent contact with Latvian modern artists who had enlisted their artistic services in the Bolshevist cause. But these very forms, especially when juxtaposed with the semi-abstract animal figuration used on the plate's rim, and coupled with the predominant earthen hues, were also intended to validate an indigenous history. From the early 1920s, the Latvian state sponsored archaeological excavations through which to "uncover" a pre-Slavic (and pre-Teutonic) nativism. The deer form and the earth tonalities of the decorative "sections" of the rim might well be interpreted as furthering that objective while uniting it with an invigorating modernist visual impulse to enframe the Latvian folkloric wedding celebration.

10   See Winfried Nerdlinger, "Modernisierung, Bauhaus, Nationalsozialismus," in *Bauhaus-Moderne im Nationalsozialismus. Zwischen Anbieten und Verfolgung* (Munich: Prestel, 1993); Jonathan Petropoulos, *Artists Under Hitler: Collaboration and Survival in Nazi Germany* (New Haven, CT: Yale University Press, 2014), and K. James-Chakroborty, as in n2.

11   See, for instance, the catalogue for the exhibition shown in London, Barcelona, and Berlin (as the XXIII Council of Europe Exhibition), *Art and Power: Europe under the Dictators 1930–1945*, eds. Dawn Ades, Tim Benton, David Elliott, and Iain Boyd Whyte (London: Hayward Gallery, 1995).

12   The neologism "reactionist" is used in this volume both adjectively and adverbally in lieu of the more widely understood, if narrowly defined, terms "reactionary" or, at times "ultramontane." As is evident in the following chapters, "reactionist" ideologies, programs, and policies were variously conservative and sometimes explicitly reactionary. At other moments or on other occasions, the architects advocated attitudes that departed from an explicitly reactionary stance of some ultra-conservative politicians or ultramontane theologians.

13   At the appropriate places below, bibliographical citations for the respective figures are provided. The description of Plečnik as an "idiosyncratic modernist" derives from S. A. Mansbach, "Making the Past Modern: Jože Plečnik's Central European Landscapes in Prague and Ljubljana," in Therese O'Malley and Joachim Wolschke-Bulmahn eds., *Modernism and Landscape Architecture, 1890–1940, (Studies in the History of Art)* (Washington, DC: National Gallery of Art; Distributed by Yale University Press, 2015), pp. 95–116.

14   See Philipp Blom, *The Vertigo Years, Europe, 1900–1914* (New York: Basic Books, 2008); Peter Gay, *Schnitzler's Century: the Making of Middle-Class Culture, 1815–1914* (New York: Norton, 2002); and Carl Schorske, *Fin-de-Siècle Vienna: Politics and Culture* (New York: Random House, 1980).

15   Although the scholarly literature is far too vast to cite here, it is worth mentioning *Centropa* (January 2001–December 2015), an English-language triennial journal dedicated to *Central European Architecture and Related Arts*.

2   Progressive Architecture for a Conservative Catalonia

Lluís Domènech i Montaner, like many well-educated Catalans of the period, was both a reformer and a nationalist. He and his intellectual colleagues sought a renewal that was as much aesthetic as it was social and political. In truth, these two aspects were fundamentally plaited in the Catalan world view of the time. And they were practiced co-extensively as an effective means to achieve a national "redemption" through which the essential character, distinctive traditions, and singular identity of Catalonia could be both envisioned and actualized, especially by architects. What Domènech and his confederates most desired, and what they were popularly perceived as advancing, was a Catalonia at liberty to consolidate and assert its national distinctiveness, essentially independent artistically and politically from an "imperial" definition of national integrity promoted from Madrid and undergirded by a confining Augustan authority of classicism.[1]

What is remarkable is the leading role assumed by architects in drawing the plans for a *Catalunya nova*. For, as we shall shortly see, Domènech i Montaner, Josep Puig i Cadafalch (1867–1956),[2] and others assumed positions of political and administrative leadership at the highest levels. In a manner almost without parallel,[3] these figures designed the architecture of and for a *modernista* Catalonia in both a literal and political sense, assuming the mantle of administrative office as architects of the Catalan spirit. Although other artists in their orbit enjoyed public regard and professional respect, most notably Antoni Gaudí (1852–1926), few recognized political office as an efficacious extensive of their architectural practice.[4]

The renaissance of Catalonian self-identity and cultural assertiveness was originally apolitical. Attracting liberals and conservatives, most based in Barcelona, which was undergoing an economic boom in the third quarter of the 19th century, the *Renaixença* was initially a literary movement. Although foreshadowed by the 1833 publication in Catalan of the alexandrine *Oda a la Pàtria* by Bonaventura Carles Aribau i Farriols (1798–1862), the cultural movement might most conveniently be understood as dating from 1859 with the revival of the Jocs Florals, vastly popular poetry competitions in Catalan based on (romanticized) medieval models. Within the next 20 years, the cultural movement had been consolidated through the founding of the journal *La Renaixença* (1871) by the Catalan poet Jacint Verdaguer i Santaló and Barcelona-born author and politician Victor Balaguer i Cirera, and, in 1879, with the Catalan-language daily, *Diari Català* initiated by Valentí Almirall i Llozer.[5] All shared an abiding faith in a regional nationalism that exalted Catalonia's medieval greatness and celebrated its contemporary economic potency as the industrial and commercial center of Iberia. Admittedly, Barcelona's long history as a port and entrepôt positioned it ideally to export its industrial products to Spain's overseas colonies, which proved a ready market for Catalonia's extensive and technologically advanced textile industry. It was the factory production of inexpensive cloth that proved the bedrock of the cultural and national renaissance, just as it furnished the means and men that would allow for the first phase of *modernisme*.

The formative link between industry and culture increasingly lent the *Renaixença* a conservative political character. Of course, not all those who promoted the codification of Catalan grammar and the employment of the "national" language for both high art and quotidian purposes were conservatives. There were adherents to *Renaixença*'s late Romantic nature who advocated forms of republicanism (most notably against the centralizing and monarchical Spanish state). Nonetheless, a supervening Catalan nationalism, ranging from cultural independence to political autonomy, united those whose world view veered from ultramontanism to liberalism and most intermediary points on the spectrum. Increasingly, architecture was called upon to provide an appropriate form for the revival of regional pride and distinctiveness. And Domènech fulfilled these expectations, first ideologically and then visually.

Between 1877 and 1879, Domènech made apparent his nationalist ambitions through the publication of his two seminal essays in (and his design for the masthead of) *La Renaixença* (spelled Renaxensa in those years), the organ of the cultural society. This marked the high point of the movement, just as it presaged the rise of its far richer and more consequent successor, *modernisme*, for which Domènech would constitute the decisive pillar. Of his early writings, "Comments on the Exhibition of the Sumptuary Arts" and "In Search of a National

Architecture,"[6] both published in this seminal periodical of Catalan cultural revivalism, the latter is pivotal. Here, in impassioned prose Domènech articulated the guiding principles for and provided a compelling rationalization of a national and modern architecture for his native Catalonia.[7] Having already declared in the earlier essay the necessity of studying "everything: from the most primitive works to the latest manifestations" by which to "give us new life when injected in our veins,"[8] the architect-theorist exhorted his professional colleagues to privilege the role of the national idea over the traditional preoccupation with materials and processes. Domènech avers that the current conditions of modern society are ripe for architecture to aspire to a truly national character with its own type of construction, its own forms of ornamentation,[9] and its own stylistic currency. "Never before has the climate been so right" for Catalans to "be inspired by their own national traditions." Hence, contemporary architects, their patrons, and their public need to be aware of the organizing principles of the past; but these historical precepts – and their material manifestations – cannot merely be copied by today's designers. Rather, the contemporary Catalan must recognize that "Roman art is not Roman because of where it originated; it is Roman because it represents Roman civilization."[10] Likewise, Catalonians must muster "the faith and courage" to determine for themselves a distinctive national architecture rooted in their own soil, traditions, and current circumstances. Only by creating a new, modern, and eclectic national architecture might the citizenry "lead healthy lives the way plants absorb air, water, and earth."[11]

Domènech's "Busca" essay exhorted his compatriots to see in architecture an ideological as well as an aesthetic means to construct a national individuality, one that judiciously mined the past for signs, symbols, and styles that might be reconciled to new ways of building a Catalan identity – both literally and metaphorically. At the same time, it released the nationalist movement from its bonds to an idealized past in favor of affirming the possibilities of a modern expression, characterized more by eclecticism than by historicist purity.[12] As a consequence, Domènech consolidated the association of architecture and the national essence, and he powerfully advanced the architect as the custodian of *catalanisme*. This was a practical "condominium" of commitments that would soon characterize both *modernisme* generally and the creative engagement of Domènech specifically.

Modernisme, which predominated between ca. 1880 and ca. 1910,[13] was never a carefully formulated style or a uniform philosophy. Embracing music, theater, literature, and especially the visual arts, it

might best be comprehended as a medley of inventive modes and political orientations, all drawing inspiration from the past, by which to
create a national Catalan culture fit for a modern age.[14] As a visual cor-
ollary to the revival of the Catalan language, *modernista* architecture
was to a degree an accommodation with other progressive movements
in Europe but without sacrificing local particularities.[15] Ideologically,
it was cosmopolitan and very much the expression of the industrial
and urban elite which sought a material reflection of their financial authority and commercial success. As such it was most often politically
conservative even if its prime advocates shied away from embracing
explicitly any system. What was all-important was the promotion of
regional – Catalan – autonomy culturally and politically regardless
of the disparity among individual preference for republicanism, monarchy, or any other forms of government organization. Through such
events as the First Catalan Congress (1880) and the publication of *Lo
Catalanisme* (1886) by Valentí Almirall (who also founded the Centre
Català in 1883, which would protect the local textile industrial interests), for instance, Catalonia was defined in Tainian terms as a cultural
and linguistic "nation" rather than a political or geographical one.[16]

In Barcelona, *modernisme* was the manifestation of the belief in un-
fettered progress which might maximize the entire region's prosper-
ity. Given the absence of an effective economic policy from Madrid
under the restored monarchy (from 1873), the Catalan lands were at
liberty – at least until 1898 – to pursue a libertarian agenda comparatively free from social unrest.[17] In this context of flourishing industrial
development and extraordinary commercial success, based to a very
great degree on sales to and trade with Spain's overseas colonies, principally Cuba and the Philippines, architects were afforded unprecedented prospects to build. Moreover, they were encouraged by their
cultural engagement to assume political responsibilities as well. And
no one was better positioned to capitalize on both opportunities than
Lluís Domènech.

At the age of 19 (1869), Domènech had enrolled as a founding member in the first "Catalanista" political society, "La Jove Catalunya."[18]
His early activity would presage his long engagement with politics and
Catalan culture. Within a few years, he affiliated with the Lliga de
Catalunya through which he would eventually consolidate his political
ascendency and ultimately become what many have acknowledged as
the most outstanding personality of political Catalanism of the age.[19]
The Lliga was the political arm of a powerful group of conservative industrialists, politicians, and architects who sought to safeguard both
local financial and cultural interests against any encroachment from

the central state. As part of his commitment to further the study of Catalonia's history, art, and archaeology, and as a patron of contemporary Catalan literati, Domènech combined his explicitly political activities at the time with more general cultural ones, such as his years as president of the Jocs Florals de Barcelona poetry competitions. Nonetheless, by the early 1890s, when the Lliga de Catalunya had devolved into the Unió Catalanista (1891), Domènech was elected as its president. At its first major congress, which took place in the city hall of the geographically central town of Manresa in March 1892, the so-called *Bases de Manresa* was promulgated. Through this document, which demanded federal autonomy for Catalonia, *political catalisme* was asserted.[20] Domènech secured partial Spanish support for several of the Manresa articles, at least until 1899 when there was a change in the Spanish government. The makeup of the Spanish Cortes shifted in the election of 1899 with the electoral victory of Domènech and his party (and their various Catalonian political allies). Nonetheless, and despite the political success, the architect began to distance himself from the Unió Catalanista and soon joined the Centre Nacional Català, where he could advocate more forcefully his belief in a predominantly cultural *catalisme* over the political principles set forth in the *Bases de Manresa*. In the new formation, Domènech continued to play a leading role, again one characterized by an abiding conservative orientation in which the *bürgerliche* interests of Barcelona's upper classes were fostered as the most effective means of consolidating a modern Catalonian identity. Yet, whether as a result of political exhaustion or as a sign of his belief in the primacy of architecture as the most efficacious way of advancing the national culture of Catalunya, Domènech began to step aside from his many political offices, though not before helping to set the stage for the triumph of Catalan forces in the April 1905 local elections.[21] Around 1904, he had grown increasingly disenchanted with the practice (if not the ideology) of politics and was eager to devote his energies principally to building. By the time he renounced his political offices in 1906,[22] he had embarked on his two greatest architectural works, each of which would represent a creative triumph for its maker as well as constitute a hallmark for the *modernista* Catalan nation.[23]

Domènech's narrowing of focus to the cultural realm may be attributed in part to personality. Admittedly, he was not a "natural" politician. He was reserved, quiet, and often irascible; moreover, he disliked the politician's reliance on cajoling and remonstrating. As he remarked in letters to his professional colleagues, he felt most comfortable conducting solitary research into native archaeology and regional history, as well as architectural and art history; in pursuing bookbinding and carrying out graphic design; in delivering academic lectures; or, especially, in practicing architecture. His many years as director of the school of architecture, president of the Barcelona Ateneu, and other cultural leadership positions more than satisfied any interest in administration.[24] And yet, for more than a decade during his most productive years, he allowed himself to be elected to high political party office. From these illustrious posts, he consistently and effectively promoted conservative economic and social programs, while passionately advancing progressive cultural causes – all with the intention of realizing a modern Catalunya worthy of its past and deserving of its future.

It is in his architecture – especially in those major undertakings from the first dozen years of the 20th century – that one can best witness Domènech's aesthetic originality. In the Palau de la Música Catalana (1905–1908) and in the Hospital de la Santa Creu i Sant Pau (1902–1912), in particular, Domènech achieved an inventiveness of form, a creative use of materials and of construction methods, and an emblematic design that must be counted among the most imaginative, compelling, and progressive of the entire era universally (Figures 2.1 and 2.2).[25]

The Palace of Music was a materialization of the national ideology. Rooted in the cultural matrix of the *Renaixença*, the formative impulse was a mid-century appreciation of Catalan choral music, especially singing. Josep Anselm Clavé i Camps (1824–1874), a poet, composer, and – typically – conservative politician, united his enthusiasms by creating a choir for working-class men in the middle of the 19th century. He, like so many of his compatriots, believed in the power of culture to create an abiding and genuine regional reality. Significantly, he focused these efforts less on high art, such as the musical medium of opera that would become essential to the *modernistas*, than on the simple harmonies and popular songs that the unschooled lower class might master and authentically embrace as its own.[26] With the supersession of the *Renaixença* by *modernisme*, the choirs became increasingly middle class, thereby reflecting the interests and patronage of the elite. By the early 1890s, moreover, the men's chorus (*Orfeó*, as it was known locally) was enriched by sections for women and for children in an effort to harmonize singing with the breadth of Barcelona's population. As was common practice, culture and politics were deeply connected. The "Orfeó Catalanà," formed in 1891 under the baton of the composer and conductor Lluís Millet i Pagès (1867–1941), was underwritten in part by the Lliga Catalunya.[27] After a peripatetic

Figure 2.1 Lluís Domènech i Montaner, *Palau de la Música Catalana* (1905–1908). Source: Photograph courtesy of Professor Antoni Bover Tanyà and Miquel Bigas Tañà of the Universitat Politècnica de Catalunya (CITM) and La Farinera, Centre d'Arts Visuals de Vic.

existence, the society secured a building site in 1904 on the Carrer Sant Pere Més Alt and immediately contracted with Domènech for an appropriate design through which to signal the political maturity of Catalan culture.

It is important to remark on the site itself; for its urban setting reveals much about the history, purpose, and symbolism of the Palau. Unlike many other national music venues, the Palau's location foreclosed

Figure 2.2 Lluís Domènech i Montaner, *Hospital de la Santa Creu i Sant Pau* (1902–1912).
Source: Photograph courtesy of Professor Antoni Bover Tanyà and Miquel Bigas Tañà of the Universitat Politècnica de Catalunya (CITM) and La Farinera, Centre d'Arts Visuals de Vic.

the possibility of a heroic pedestrian perspective or a stately progress toward a looming building in the distance (Figure 2.1). In contrast, Vienna's Hofoper (later Staatsoper) or Paris's Opéra (originally the Salle des Capucines) by Charles Garnier (both 1860s and 1870s) were sited so that the approach would impress passersby with the heroic scale of the national (musical and balletic) institution and the city that displayed it to monumental effect. Thus, the buildings' facades were scaled and oriented to viewpoints both along a grand avenue and from a plaza or open space before the main facade. Barcelona's Palau was hemmed in by a working-class district, and hence afforded no theatrical approach, no dramatic revelation of a massive facade, and no "forecourt" in which crowds might congregate before a symbol of the nation's cultural triumph (Figure 2.1). Rather, the building was embedded in the very social context in which Clavé's utopian-minded belief in working-class choruses might be ideally anchored. The Palau's exterior thus reveals itself gradually and often surprisingly, rewarding the viewer with glimpses of details rather than with a visual comprehension of the whole.

It is almost to have been expected that Domènech would have been awarded the commission in 1904 when he was at the acme of his career as both politician and architect. His commanding stature, his long engagement with Catalan culture and its ideology, and his eagerness to step aside from political office in favor of practicing architecture made him an obvious choice. Moreover, his close working association with leading industrialists, manufacturers, and merchants made Domènech attractive as a fund raiser, as well.[28] Moreover, the general program was sufficiently vague – "a social home for the Catalan Choral Society with a large auditorium" (L'estatge social de l'Orfeó Català I una gran sala d'audicions) – to allow Domènech ample freedom. Thus, he was irresistibly attracted to this project through which he could draw on his deep knowledge of regional archaeology, sculpture, art, architecture, and music, and to capitalize on his long experience as an innovative building engineer in creating a spectacular home for, and monument to, his nation's culture.

It was not just the narrow urban location that proved challenging; the site itself was irregular.[29] This meant that ingenious solutions for the internal organization of spaces, for the circulation within and between inside and outside of the building, and for the elaborate decorative program would be necessary. And most decisively, modern means of construction, use of contemporary materials, and a progressive organization of labor forces would need to be combined with the invocation of symbolic references that might resonate regionally and reverberate internationally. By reconciling domestic expectations with modern European practices, Domènech both celebrated the singularity of his nation while affirming its connections to other advanced societies. It was an ideological aspiration that paralleled his creative balance between industrial steel construction and handcrafted, traditional ornamentation in stucco, stone, enamel, and colored glass. Such duality required flexibility, and Domènech was constantly making changes to his plans during construction, especially as he confronted the challenges of the awkward site and as he worked with teams of decorators, craftsmen, and artists. Instead of seeing these alterations as the architect's lack of absolute control, it would be more accurate to recognize them as acts of creative evolution or a mode of generative originality.

The Palau is entered from the Carrer de Sant Pere Més Alt through a double vaulted portico (Figure 2.1). Originally, one side was left open and reserved for automobiles, while the other had protective glass and was intended for pedestrians. A highly ornamented pier divides the two at the street intersection. From its stuccoed upper reaches, where long balconies run along the building's two principal facades, is a massive ensemble of sculpted figures by Miquel Blay that collectively personify Catalan Song. Although the complexity of the grouping is difficult to see, and almost impossible to comprehend from the street, given the absence of adequate spatial distance, the symbolic import is reiterated by busts of composers which sit atop buttresses that spring from columns encrusted with colorful tiling. Near the top of the principal facade is a large allegorical depiction in mosaic of the songsters belonging to the Orfeó Català, which despite the size of the representation also cannot be seen from the street. Much of the elaborate and carefully planned external ornamentation is thus unable to be picked out by the pedestrian. Yet, the effect is one of visual splendor and psychical energy, as colorful patterns, rich materials, and undulating sculpture enliven the experience of passing by or, equally important, prepares one for a deepening of the sensorial experience upon entering. But before passing through the portal, one will have been sensitized to the remarkable use of materials.

The extraordinary complexity of the ornamentation on the two exterior facades is effectively juxtaposed with the clarity provided by Domènech's use of brick, a hallowed regional building material. Large surface areas of reddish brick offer visual relief from the polychromed embellishment. But these expanses also function as effective backgrounds over which the play of swirling mosaics, cascading stucco drapery, dangling sculpted figures, and exuberantly floreating capitals are both highlighted and kept proportionally in check.[30] As a result, the architecture attains a creative tension between structure and ornamentation, between control and exuberance, and between contemporaneous building practice and symbolic references (Figure 2.3).

Excited by the exterior, one is becalmed by entering the lobby through a wood and glass partition. The space itself is generously open and surrounded by a yellow tiled dado. Moving forward, one soon encounters a few steps that lead to a double staircase. Should one elect to ignore the staircase and walk forward, one would then descend a few more steps to enter a large and richly decorated patrons' café. Above both the café and lobby, and reached by the double staircase with its glass-clad twisted steel bars, is a richly decorated landing leading to the concert hall itself. The view into the concert hall has been rightly

Figure 2.3 Lluís Domènech i Montaner, *Palau de la Música Catalana* (1905–1908). Source: Photograph courtesy of Professor Antoni Bover Tanyà and Miquel Bigas Tañà of the Universitat Politècnica de Catalunya (CITM) and La Farinera, Centre d'Arts Visuals de Vic.

described as affording "one of world architecture's [sic] most uplifting experiences (Figures 2.4 and 2.5)."[31]

Although often praised since its creation as one of the most magnificent concert halls ever built, its visual splendor (and acoustic accomplishment) should not blind one to its extraordinary aesthetic inventiveness and engineering originality. It may not be unreasonable to think that the architect had in mind the adages of two of his favorite authors from his extensive library of German thinkers, poets, and critics: Friedrich von Schelling's claim that "Architecture is music in space, as if it were frozen music" and Johann Wolfgang von Goethe's poetic assertion that "Music is liquid architecture; architecture is frozen music." Nevertheless, Domènech was aiming for even more than literary allusion. In the Palau's concert hall, he created a rectangular room with a lavishly tiled ceiling, soaring windows surrounding three of the four walls, columns festooned with parti-colored tiles and surmounted by dazzling light fixtures, and additional supports akin to colored fan vaults. Of all this splendor, each uplifting the spirit of the listener and all made possible by the steel curtain wall that holds up the large hall, several additional features need to be mentioned. First,

Figure 2.4 Lluís Domènech i Montaner, *Palau de la Música Catalana* (1905–1908).
Source: Photograph courtesy of Professor Antoni Bover Tanyà and Miquel Bigas Tañà
of the Universitat Politècnica de Catalunya (CITM) and La Farinera, Centre d'Arts
Visuals de Vic.

there is the enormous stained glass central skylight (by Antoni Rigalt),
whose prominent convex centerpiece depends dramatically. Second,
and equally impressive, is the ensemble that constitutes the prosce-
nium and the rounded back wall of the performance stage. The arch
over the stage presents a host of sculpted figures executed by Dídac
Masana and Pau Gargallo. To the right is depicted the "ride of the
Valkyries" beneath which is a double Doric entablature, and between
the two Doric columns is a bust of Beethoven. On the left under spread-
ing branches is a giant bust of Josep Clavé beneath which a group of
stylish Catalan maidens either holds a lamb, caresses long tresses, or
holds down the long swag of braided flowers that depends from the
area of the portrait bust.[32] This harmonization of differences in national reference and in relief is also beautifully expressed on the stage's
concave back wall. Arrayed in a semicircle are the figures of 18 young
women interwoven into two "floating" tiers. Metaphorically, they in-
habit two realms, the spiritual and the erotic, just as they exist literally

Figure 2.5 Lluís Domènech i Montaner, *Palau de la Música Catalana* (1905–1908).
Source: Photograph courtesy of Professor Antoni Bover Tanyà and Miquel Bigas Tañã of the Universitat Politècnica de Catalunya (CITM) and La Farinera, Centre d'Arts Visuals de Vic.

in several dimensions: the monotone upper bodies of the women protrude sculpturally from the wall (Eusebi Arnau), while their lower regions are depicted by colorful mosaics that unite with the flat wall
surface (Lluís Bru). Each of the women plays a musical instrument;
and each is dressed differently, although all wear clothing of elaborate
design. Crowning the stage, and soaring high above a large mosaic of
Catalonia's medieval escutcheon, is the organ, whose polished metal
pipes are embraced by a finely carved organ loft.[33]

In this powerful expression of Catalan cultural consciousness,
Domènech has ambitiously and successfully brought into conso-
nance exuberant ornament and rational geometry, emotional al-
lusions and controlled engineering, fine handwork and industrial
methods. The building had been intended from its earliest projec-
tion in the mid-19th century to its festive opening in 1908 to serve
as the fitting site where Barcelona's social classes might constitute a
new community compact through a shared Catalan culture. However, the Palau de la Música Catalana was not the only material
manifestation of the conjunction of progressive aesthetics and conservative nationalism.

The hospital complex of Santa Creu i Sant Pau was Domènech's
most elaborate and complicated architectural undertaking; it was also
the richest realization of the Catalan spirit of *modernisme*.[34] Here,
through the curative power of medicine and the redemptive authority
of progressive architecture, praxis and representation united to serve
a modernizing civil society. Domènech's hospital designs, both for
Sant Pau in Barcelona and for the Mental Institute Pere Mata in Reus
(1897–1919),[35] may be understood as a psychological antidote to the
perception of pervasive weakness and decadence that afflicted all of
Spain following the catastrophic defeat in the Spanish-American War
of 1898. The large number of casualties, the loss of economic markets for Catalonia's products and services, and the all too numerous
repatriated colonials (to an economically depressed homeland) made
the provision of enhanced medical services necessary. *Modernisme*'s
celebration of Catalan spiritual and emotional health, its affirmation
of regional industrial progress and mercantile development, and its
popular political support among all classes made it a logical format
for the largest and most modern Catalonian health facility.

The Hospital of Sant Pau was made possible through the legacy
of the Barcelona-born banker, Pau Gil i Serra (1816–1896). Although
resident in Paris where his family bank achieved signal success, Gil
remained passionately devoted to the city of his birth. Thus, upon the
dissolution of his bank, as mandated by the will, a half of the realized

profit was to be devoted to the construction of a hospital in Barcelona that should be the equal to the most advanced medical facilities to be found "in Paris, Berlin or other European capitals." The testament outlines precisely how monies are to be spent.[36] Among the will's stipulations was the formation of a commission to determine the architect through competition. The executors, however, did not feel completely bound to follow the competition committee's declared winner, as all the submissions were found lacking by the medical board constituted by the executors. As a result, the various competition boards – scientific, medical, and architectural – along with the executors themselves opted to award the commission to the one person who they argued possessed the single most distinguished social, political, and cultural credentials: Lluís Domènech i Montaner.

The project was among the most complex of the period; for it consisted of several stages, two separate hospitals, numerous medical research and provider facilities, and separate administrative and financial overseers (as well as budgets). Nonetheless, Domènech not only rose to the difficult challenges architecturally and complicated circumstances administratively, he did so while fulfilling Pau Gil's declared wishes.

For the Hospital of Sant Pau, the architect envisioned a series of pavilions embedded in a landscaped garden. This setting would contrast with the historic location of the Hospital de la Santa Creu, which occupied a medieval building in the heart of the crowded and insalubrious Gothic Quarter. The new Sant Pau hospital would instead afford its mostly impecunious patients access to the fresh air and sunshine that modern medicine advised and that accorded with John Ruskin's newly popular concept of a healthy city (here, to be understood as the network of free-standing pavilions) integrated into nature. Much of Domènech's design program was dependent on a series of real estate maneuvers, which resulted in the physical merging of the two hospitals on an elevated site in the la Sarrià district. The large plot of land eventually acquired (145,470 square meters, or 36 acres) lay in the comparatively undeveloped area just north of the Eixample, the extension of the city planned by Ildefons Cerdà in 1859 as part of the *Renaixença* urban development.[37] Given its "out-of-town" location, the city authorities needed to introduce a new street plan and lay the tracks for public transportation, the better to serve the families of the indigent patients whom Santa Creu traditionally served, and the large number of medical and support personnel necessary to staff Sant Pau.

As extensive as the changes and improvements were to the urban plan to accommodate the demands of the hospital complex, the most innovative undertakings are best found in the design of the hospitals'

pavilions and, especially their ornamentation. For here, as in the contemporaneous Palau de la Música Catalana, Domènech pursued a
totalizing vision in which *modernisme* became an efficacious prescrip-
tion for a healthy body politic.[38]

Pau Gil's will, as interpreted by its executors, mandated the construction of 12 pavilions (one for administration, one for surgery, two
for the observation of sick individuals, and eight for patient treatment).[39] By April 1901, the legal administrators of the testator, the
health department of the city, and the authorities of the various existing hospitals agreed to entrust Domènech with the commission "by
virtue of his knowledge of this type of construction and [they further]
appoint a commission to advise him composed of doctors...."[40] Within
a year, the architect had drawn up plans, secured the initial dispensa-
tion of funds, and had supervised the laying of the foundation stone of
this enormous enterprise.

The hospital complex called on all of Domènech's talents and experience: in politics and diplomacy, in engineering and structures, and in
original decorative and ornamental design. From the start, the enormous enterprise was the focus of popular attention, as it was planned
to correct the city's medical deficiencies while promoting symbolically
the cause of Catalan culture. As a result, Domènech's plans, and the
buildings' cost and style, were constant subjects of public attention.[41]
Most controversial was the architect's concept to link free-standing
pavilions, popular among advanced medical circles in late 19th-
century France and Germany, with a subterranean network of sanitary tunnels. By such an inventive use of underground connective
passages, capitalizing on the native shallow Catalan vaults,[42] he combined the virtues of a "single" medical structure with those of a dis-
tributive system of health pavilions. The subterranean transit system
allows for the easy and efficient movement of patients, staff, and sup-
plies among buildings. Moreover, the white tiled (high) wainscoting,
floors and shallow vaulted ceilings permit easy cleaning and provide
an impression of clinical sterility, a notion furthered by the periodic
sunlight-penetrating, glass-covered openings. The impression of efficiency is complimented by the engineering ingenuity through which
the water seepage into this sloping site is controlled. Moreover, the
use of steel supporting members to shore up the walls (and columns),
the remarkably innovative plumbing and "infrastructure" (sanitary,
air circulation, and heating, for instance) necessary to service widely
distributed pavilions through the underground "link" commanded
the architect's attention. Although decoration is highly restrained on
the subterranean level, one can see in the tile work, the organization of

columns where passageways intersect, and in the orchestration of light an astonishingly inventive consideration of visual effects. However, it is in and on the pavilions where decoration and engineering attain their consummation (Figure 2.6).

As with the Palau de la Música Catalana, here, too, facades and interiors of the steel-supported pavilions are cladded in red brick. Stone, mosaic, stained glass, and glazed ceramics, often in exuberantly stylized floral patterns – frequently in playful combination with a rich interplay among geometric and figurative forms – everywhere enliven surfaces. The prominence of the red and yellow *Bandera de Catalunya* (Catalan escutcheon), and of the "P" and "G" initials (for Sant Pau and for Pau Gil) are as striking as the flat tiled angels and stone sculptures that protrude from buildings' arches, pediments, balconies, and cupolas. The welter of sculpted forms, the animated facades with their syncopation of windows and richly tiled patterns and figurations, the writhing "solomonic" columns, along with the swooping balustrades and pulsating colors of the arillated rooftops – all combine for a vibrant visual experience.[43] From the colorful plantings of the gardens in which the pavilions are artfully set, through the decorated building surfaces themselves, and continuing to the

Figure 2.6 Lluís Domènech i Montaner, *Hospital de la Santa Creu i Sant Pau.*
Source: Photograph courtesy of Professor Antoni Bover Tanyà and Miquel Bigas Tañà of the Universitat Politècnica de Catalunya (CITM) and La Farinera, Centre d'Arts Visuals de Vic.

Figure 2.7 Lluís Domènech i Montaner, *Hospital de la Santa Creu i Sant Pau*.

Source: Photograph courtesy of Professor Antoni Bover Tanyà and Miquel Bigas Tañà of the Universitat Politècnica de Catalunya (CITM) and La Farinera, Centre d'Arts Visuals de Vic.

Figure 2.8 Lluís Domènech i Montaner, *Hospital de la Santa Creu i Sant Pau.*
Source: Photograph courtesy of Professor Antoni Bover Tanyà and Miquel Bigas Tañà
of the Universitat Politècnica de Catalunya (CITM) and La Farinera, Centre d'Arts
Visuals de Vic.

tops of the pavilions' cupolas, chimneys, and ridgelines, all these
"composed" levels vibrate with a life-giving force. In conformity with
Domènech's original intention and consistent with his world view,
the hospital program for Sant Pau would cure through a therapeutic
combination of the arts: medical, architectural, and the decorative
symbolic (Figures 2.7 and 2.8).

Notably, it was not only the (primarily Catalan) symbols in tile
that were used to great effect by Domènech; the making of the tiled

decoration itself was of equal consequence. Like his compatriots and contemporaries Antoni Gaudí and Josep Maria Jujol i Gibert, Domènech embraced the *trencadís*, especially for the decorative program for the Hospital Sant Pau. *Trencadís* was a favored *modernista* method of making mosaics from ceramic shards, mostly from broken dinnerware or everyday ceramic vessels. Although sometimes embraced as a "spiritual" ornamental material as well as a nationalist decorative idiom, Domènech was less likely to see in the *trencadís* a richly redemptive purpose. However, it may not be unreasonable to think that the architect recognized in his use of ceramic sherds an appropriately politicized embellishment, as its use was widely acknowledged since the end of the 19th century as an essentially Catalan practice (Figure 2.9).[44]

Figure 2.9 Lluís Domènech i Montaner, *Hospital de la Santa Creu i Sant Pau.*
Source: Photograph courtesy of Professor Antoni Bover Tanyà and Miquel Bigas Tañà of the Universitat Politècnica de Catalunya (CITM) and La Farinera, Centre d'Arts Visuals de Vic.

Most of the treatment pavilions feature a high dome through which filtered light can enter the large wards. The dome artfully conceals water storage tanks, just as the supporting walls hide the intermural space for natural cooling.[45] The desired dependence on mostly natural cooling is primarily reliant on the double tier of windows, the upper row of which can be blocked by lowering wooden shades. By contrast, some of the heating elements are placed down the center of the long ward, the better to maximize radiating warmth during the winter. Waste water pipes are carefully set into channels or interstices both to avoid contamination and to optimize efficiency. Domènech was particularly conscientious in his consideration of sanitary facilities, especially regarding bodily evacuation and the disposal of soiled dressings, as these had been serious liabilities at the Hospital de la Santa Creu in its medieval facility. As a result, the pavilions were equipped with the most up-to-date sanitary installations, from water closets to sinks to the extensive use of easily scrubbed surface tiling. The principal wards were capacious, thereby avoiding unhealthy crowding, but also permitting a salubrious sense of semi-privacy as well as ensuring the flexibility that individual medical treatment might require. In sum, the technical aspects of the program required the same degree of inventiveness and originality as the decorative components. Each was understood by the architect, the medical boards, and Barcelona's public as a necessary reagent in creating a *modernista* Catalan reaction (Figure 2.10).

The demands of such a large and complex medical facility taxed Domènech's energies. This may help to explain why he stepped aside from his formal political offices as the hospital was in its initial construction phase around 1904–1905.[46] Moreover, at the same time, the Palau de la Música Catalana was commanding the architect's attention.[47] These circumstances must have persuaded the former chairman (or commissioner) of the Lliga de Catalunya, the Unió Catalanista, the Bases de Manresa, the Centre Nacional Català, and the Lliga Regionalista to husband his resources for architecture, a discipline he had always recognized as the most potent means of building and conserving a Catalan identity. But one might adduce a further reason why Domènech may have felt that he could step aside now from explicit political engagement in order to focus on his architectural commissions. In his circle of close professional associates, both political and architectural, he recognized the signal talents and passionate commitments of Josep Puig i Cadafalch.[48] Puig more than anyone working with Domènech evinced the same creative combination of conservative

Figure 2.10 Lluís Domènech i Montaner, *Hospital de la Santa Creu i Sant Pau*.

Source: Photograph courtesy of Professor Antoni Bover Tanyà and Miquel Bigas Tañà of the Universitat Politècnica de Catalunya (CITM) and La Farinera, Centre d'Arts Visuals de Vic.

political action and aesthetic progressivism. In Puig, Domènech must have felt he had a true colleague in whose hands he could entrust their shared views of Catalan culture and politics.

The younger architect focused assiduously on the elder's world view with a genuine sympathy for his political accomplishments and the (implied) ideological aspirations they shared. Already in 1902 Puig had published a lengthy article (in Spanish) on Domènech.[49] As a *modernista* architect and designer, Puig had previously demonstrated his bona fides, perhaps most effectively in his *Casa Antoni Amatller*

(1900) on the main street of the Eixample,[50] and almost immediately thereafter in the impressive *La Casa de les Punxes* (1903–1905). Further parallels between the two figures can be drawn biographically, politically, and architecturally. As was the case with Domènech, Puig too was deeply engrossed in the study of the Catalonian past with particular interest in its distinguished archaeology, architecture, sculpture, and decorative arts.[51] This led him, as it did for Domènech, to participate in the nationalist poetry competitions organized by the Jocs Florals for which he designed a throne for the victor. Moreover, like Domènech he had studied the sciences as well as the arts, having taken a degree in physics and mathematics. At a relatively youthful age, he joined the Unió Catalanista, a conservative political formation of which Domènech was president. In his architectural work of the period, he readily pursued a *modernista* practice of enlisting and organizing a small army of craftsmen and artisans, many the same who worked for Domènech.[52] Likewise, he authored articles for both the culturally progressive and politically conservative *La Renaixença* and *La Veu de Catalunya* [The Voice of Catalonia].[53] But it is in his more explicit political activities where the parallels might best be recognized. Puig participated in the negotiations that resulted in the *Bases de Manresa* to which Domènech's presence had been crucial, and this helped propel him into the highest circles of Catalan nationalist politics and culture (Figure 2.11).

Groomed politically and inspired architecturally by Domènech, Puig continued to refine his skills through a series of major architectural and planning commissions and by means of numerous administrative posts within the medley of conservative Lligas that governed Barcelona and much of Catalonia. The acme arrived in April 1914. In this month, the Mancomunitat de Catalunya (the Commonwealth of Catalonia) was legally established and officially recognized by the Spanish royal government.[54] Even though it was restricted principally to administrative functions, it represented the first recognition by the centralized state of the existence and of the unity of Catalonia since the year 1714. The political authority of the Mancomunitat was the Lliga Regionalista of which Domènech had once been president. Its current leader was the retired president's confederate Enric Prat de la Riba and ably assisted by Josep Puig i Cadafalch, who would soon assume the presidency himself. Under Puig's leadership, the Commonwealth consolidated the intertwined cultural and political aspirations that had motivated Catalan architects to create the monuments of the *Renaixença* and *modernisme*.[55] In both a symbolic and concrete sense, Puig's administration was the fulfillment of the

Figure 2.11 Josep Puig i Cadafalch, *La Casa de les Punxes* (House of Spikes) or *Casa Terradas*, (1903–1905).

Source: Photograph courtesy of Professor Antoni Bover Tanyà and Miquel Bigas Tañà of the Universitat Politècnica de Catalunya (CITM) and La Farinera, Centre d'Arts Visuals de Vic.

ambitions that Domènech i Montaner and his allies had so long promoted in word, brick, and deed.[56]

Paradoxically, the triumph of an explicitly Catalan ideology coincided with the diminishing authority of *modernisme* as a "style" or aesthetic program. Beginning around 1906 and increasingly by 1910, *noucentisme* [*nou* meaning both "nine" and "new" in Catalan, as in the "1900s" and "new century," the term coined in 1906 by Eugeni d'Ors] was ascendant. Part of this successor movement's popularity can be attributed to its preservation and advocacy of the same nationalist objectives and conservative politics that lay at the center of, first, the *Renaixença* and then, far more potently, *modernisme*. Yet aesthetically, *noucentisme* promoted a rather practical, and at times institutional, accommodation with the prevailing authorities. This was, of course, made easier politically by the sympathy of the local Barcelona and regional Catalonian governments, which were dominated mostly by the Lliga Regionalista. However, the movement was also favored by a public (and a patron class) increasingly captivated by a Mediterranean neo-classicism. The highly individualistic buildings of *modernisme* were seen increasingly as radical departures from a European mainstream of classical order and relative restraint. Moreover, with the triumph of the *modernista* ideology, coupled with the moderation that the Mancomunitat sought to institute, an architecture of extreme individualism was no longer recognized as necessary or even desirable to achieve a Catalan cultural identity.[57] Rather, it was the classicizing *noucentisme* that would mark the conclusion of the most intense, inventive, and exciting braiding of architecture, conservatism, and nationalism in Catalonia. As a result, we must turn our attention elsewhere to encounter another creative conjunction of progressive aesthetics and reactionist ideology through which to refine our understanding of the formative phases of modernism.

Notes

1   The role of antiquity would become a defining characteristic of how the Catalan architects and Plečnik creatively and selectively embraced the distant past in their respective attempts to forge a national identity free from the Roman classicism that each associated with an imposed "imperial" authority, respectively Spanish, and Austro-Hungarian. See below.

2   Although stylistically Josep Maria Jujol i Gibert (1879–1949) must be included among the talented cohort of *modernistas*, especially for his creative work under and with Gaudí, Jujol was comparatively less explicitly engaged politically than many of his architect confederates. He did share the conservative cultural and political outlook of Gaudí, as well as supported the programs of the conservative-nationalist Lliga Regionalista party led by Domènech. Nonetheless, his 20 years as a municipal architect in a small provincial Catalonian town and his long career as a liturgical architect took precedence. See José Llinàs and Jordi Sarrà, *Josep Maria Jujol*, (Cologne: Taschen 1992 and 2007) and Mariàngels Fondevila, "The Extravagant Jujol," in *Barcelona and Modernity: Picasso, Gaudí, Miró, Dalí* (New Haven, CT: Yale University Press, for the Cleveland Museum of Art, 2007).

3   Many of the classical modernists aspired to shape the social and political fabric of their native lands – as well as exercise universal impact. Indeed, at the very core of modernist ideology was a belief in the redemptive

power of art, primarily abstraction, as the most effective means to effect fundamental change. Yet with the exception of the isolated and very limited cases of Hungarian avant-gardists during the short-lived Republic of Councils in 1919 and of the circumscribed authority (which was more pedagogical than explicitly political) of Malevich and Chagall in Vitebsk about the same time, there were no architects or artists who were afforded the political opportunities of the Catalans, especially between roughly 1890 and 1923. Among those who held important social or political positions, in addition to Domènech and Puig who are addressed in this essay, one may note Joan Rubió i Bellver (1870–1952), who served as a *regidor* (councilor) on the Barcelona City Council (Ajuntament de Barcelona) in 1905; and Josep Maria Pericas (1881–1965), whose social and political engagement would take place mostly in the 1930s.

4   Gaudí's social and political world view has been the principal focus of both researchers and the general public. By contrast, Domènech (and his confederates, especially Puig) had long been dismissed in the non-Catalonian scholarship. The originality of their work, their potent politics, and the influence they would exert on later art movements had been mostly overlooked until the beginning of the current century. Henry Russell Hitchcock had dismissed Domènech, for instance, in his magisterial *Architecture: Nineteenth and Twentieth Centuries* (Baltimore, MD: Penguin Books, 1958; second ed. 1963; fourth ed., Harmondsworth, UK and New York: Penguin Books, 1977). Serious scholarly attention in the English-speaking world was inaugurated with the pioneering doctoral dissertation by Judith Campbell Rohrer, *Artistic Regionalism and Architectural Politics in Barcelona, c.1880–c.1906*, (Ph.D. diss., Columbia University, 1984). Nonetheless, there was a delay of almost a decade before others continued Rohrer's pursuits.

5   There is an extensive Spanish and Catalan literature on the *Renaixença*. English-language studies are comparatively few, the plurality of which are to be found in chapters to anthologies, articles in professional journals (most consistently, the *Catalan Journal of Communication & Cultural Studies*), and exhibition catalogs (containing essays such as Francesc Fontbona, "The Renaixença in Art" or Jordi Falgàs's "Greeting the Dawn: The Impact of the Renaixença in Periodicals and Architecture," both in *Barcelona and Modernity*, as in n2).

6   Domènech, "Á propòsit de la exposició d'Arts suntuarias," (Regarding the Exhibition of Sumptuary Arts) in *La Renaxensa: periódich de literatura, ciencias y arts*, tome II, year VII, no. 10, 31 October 1877, pp. 292–303; Ibid., "En busca de una arquitectura nacional," in *La Renaixensa*, 28 February 1878, year VIII, number 4, vol. 1, pp. 149–60. The publication of Domènech's two articles is linguistically noteworthy. The first, on sumptuary arts, bears both title and text in Catalan, as one would expect in this vigorously culturally nationalistic journal. However, his major theoretical text for the arts, "In Search of a National Architecture," has a Spanish title and a Catalan text. [See the Appendix for the first English translation.] Here, it is possible that the architect was seeking to convince a larger, extra-Catalonian audience of the need for a Catalan national architecture, especially as a full Spanish translation was soon available. Surely, he would have been familiar with similar calls by architects throughout

Europe, especially French and German figures whose works he visited and whose original writings he read fluently. See n9 and n32.

7   Domènech had first studied the natural sciences, engineering, and the classics in Barcelona before moving to Madrid to enroll in the Escuela Especial de Arquitectura during the years 1870–1873. Although he was awarded the Prix de Rome, he was compelled by the sudden death of his father to decline the honor and return to his home, where he began his life-long engagement with Catalonian history and archaeology, as well as with the visual arts in general. By the mid-1870s, he was teaching at the Escuela d'Arqitectura de Barcelona (founded in 1872 but not officially recognized until 1875), where he spent 45 years, 20 of which as its director. For much of this time, especially between 1889 and 1904, Domènech was deeply engaged in politics. See below.

8   See Lourdes Figueras i Borrull, *Lluís Domènech i Montaner* (Barcelona: Editiones de Belloch, second revised edition, 2007), pp. 209–11.

9   For Domènech, as for many architects of the time in France, England, and Germany, ornament was a primary concern. Although it is unlikely that either John Ruskin's or William Morris's writings were widely known in Spain before 1900 (see Rohrer, *Artistic Regionalism*, p. 161), Viollet-le-Duc's theories were familiar to Catalan architects and designers; and Domènech mentions the Frenchmen explicitly in his essay ("Busca," p. 156). Moreover, the Catalan had traveled through Germany and much of Austria; and in Vienna he would have come across the work of Gottfried Semper, an architect whose theories the Barcelona architect admired. Domènech's personal library contained a large number of German-language architectural treatises, illustrated books, and design manuals, many of which treated ornament directly.

10   "L'art romà no és romà pel lloc del seu origen, ho és per representar la civilització romana." See the Appendix (p. 74) for the full context of the quotation, which is more widely known in its Spanish translation, "El arte romano no es romano por el lugar de su origen, lo es por representar la civilización romana."

11   Translation is by the author. For the full context of this passage, see the Appendix (pp. 78–79). There are several studies of the text, among the more penetrating is that by Lluís Domènech i Girbau in "The Architect and the Spirit of the Time," in *L'arquitecte Lluís Domènech i Montaner* (Palma and Lleida: Fondació "la Caixa," 1996).

12   The present discussion admittedly does not put sufficient emphasis on the role of eclecticism for Domènech's world view during the late 1870s. It was important for the architect to make a case for borrowing from many past epochs and cultural sources, especially in developing ornament. Toward that end, he addressed in the "Busca" various methods of eclectic borrowing, which he acknowledged as "respectable." Further, eclecticism allowed him to draw liberally from ancient to medieval to Romantic building types and examples in an overarching attempt to construct a Catalan style appropriate for the modern age. In his comparative free-wheeling advocacy and practice, he began to liberate himself from the *Renaixença* absorption with Catalonia's medieval monuments as emblematic of the "principality's" greatness: spiritually, commercially, and visually. By the late 1870s, the attraction of the local past, especially the

widely Romanticized 13th-century reign of Jaume (James) I, Count of Barcelona and King of Aragon, began to diminish, a shift attributable, in significant measure, to Domènech's activity as essayist, architect, and budding politician.

13   According to Rohrer, *Artistic Regionalism*, the term was first used by progressive figures associated with the journal *L'Avenç* (1884–1893), in its inaugural "Declaration of Purpose" [Declaració de Propòsit] (first issue), and also with the periodical *La Vanguardia*. She argues (p. 22) that *modernisme* as a form does not apply "to any of those Barcelona architects whom we have come to consider almost automatically as such." She bases her assertion on the claim that Modernism in Catalonia rejected the past, whereas the regionalist architects maintained an emotional link to a Golden Age. The current essay does not follow or endorse the reservations expressed by Rohrer, in particular her juxtaposition of Catalanists – to whom she attributes a progressive modernity (p. 72) – and *modernistas* – to whom she assigns a conservativism rooted in retrospection (p. 73). I do, however, readily acknowledge that Rohrer's dissertation was the first scholarly study to investigate the rich reliance between architecture and politics by examining the articles and speeches in the political and popular press. Although her views have been refined and slightly modified in her later writings, such as those devoted to Gaudí and Puig, the perspective advanced in the dissertation remains a touchstone for current studies even as her claims have been respectfully contested, as in the current study.

14   For a helpful summary of *modernisme*'s "mentality," see Vincenç Villatoro, "El *Modernismo* Catalán como Movimento Social," in *El Hospital de la Santa Creu i Sant Pau, 1401–2001*, (coordinated by Lourdes Figueras and Maria Manadé), (Madrid: Lunwerg Editores, 2001), pp. 77–84.

15   For many years, *modernisme* has been described as a Catalonian version of Art Nouveau or Jugendstil. But in almost every respect, from the aesthetic to the ideological and from the perspective of its makers to that of its audiences, there is little justification for such a claim despite selective use of floral forms, and a chronological coincidence between the expression of a popular visual culture in Barcelona and that in Brussels, Riga, Vienna, Turin, and elsewhere. For a succinct description of *modernisme*'s differences from international Art Nouveau, see O. Bohigas, "The Life and Works of a Modernista Architect," in *Domènech i Montaner Año 2000*, (Barcelona: Col.legi d'Arquitectes de Catalunya, Centre de Documentoció, 2000), p. 24.

16   It is important to understand the political context of these claims and events. With the Bourbon restoration in 1873, Madrid sought to affirm the political and geographical unity of Spain; hence, the stance taken by Almirall and his cultural confederates may be recognized as juxtaposing Catalan and Spanish identities.

17   According to Chris Ealham, *Class, Culture and Conflict in Barcelona: 1898–1937* (London and New York: Routledge, 2005, p. 34), Catalonia had only a weak social democratic movement, especially after 1899 when the General Workers' Union, the dominant socialist trade union, decamped Barcelona for Madrid. In its wake, and not unlike many other cities in Europe of the time, anarchism assumed the principal oppositional "movement" to the well-established bourgeoisie. Barcelona endured a spate of anarchist bombings during the 1890s and at least two general strikes, in 1902 and 1909.

18   See M. Coll i Alentorn, "Historical Background," in *Domènech i Montaner Año 2000*, p. 16.

19   Ibid., p. 18.

20   After the first point, acknowledging areas in which the Spanish state is predominant, 16 further articles ("bases") are enumerated through which the powers reserved for Catalunya are articulated. These include all those areas affecting language, cultural traditions, local government and laws, and so forth. Article 12, which addresses the nature and limitations of Catalonia's contribution to the state's army and navy, would become highly controversial. The eventual abrogation of the *Bases de Manresa*, especially regarding this specific article, would have dramatic consequences in the violence of the 1909 *la Setmana Tràgica*, a week-long series of bloody confrontations between the Spanish army and the working classes of Barcelona (and other cities of Catalonia), backed mostly by anarchists, with the participation of some republicans. The violence was precipitated by the call-up of reserve troops by Prime Minister Antonio Maura to be sent as reinforcements when Spain renewed military activity in its Moroccan colony in early July 1909. The destruction in Barcelona was extensive, including the torching of numerous churches, monasteries, and religiously affiliated buildings mostly by anti-clerical anarchists.

21   The elections were the first victory for the newly formed Lliga Regionalista, a conservative Catalanist political party with a monarchist wing. It enjoyed wide support among the middle class. It was constituted in 1901 through the merger of two political groups, the Unió Regionalista and the Centre Nacional Català, both traditionally conservative and nationalist, and both guided by the political skills of Domènech. The new party's press organ was *La Veu de Catalunya* (The Voice of Catalonia), founded in 1899. Among the most notable figures in the party was Enric Prat de la Riba i Sarrà (1870–1917), a conservative politician who was widely admired as the author of *La nacionalitat catalana* (1906) in which he asserted a distinctive Catalan art parallel to that of the Catalan language, and whose party leadership was followed by that of the architect of *catalanisme* – and both a disciple of Domènech and a working confederate of Gaudí – Josep Puig i Cadafalch (discussed below).

22   By this date, Domènech's reluctance to continue his explicitly political activities was shared by other artists, especially those affiliated with the Lliga Regionalista, who recognized the limitations of their ideological partisanship to sustain wide support, and, in particular, the sympathies of the right-wing groups with which they had long collaborated. See Rohrer, *Artistic Regionalism*, p. 320.

23   The Hospital de la Santa Creu i Sant Pau and the Palau de la Música Catalana, projects he initiated between 1900 and 1912, and discussed below, can rightly be hailed as Domènech's greatest works. Nonetheless, it is important to recognize that he had been active as a well-recognized architect for more than 20 years. From at least 1888, he had secured an international reputation as a major Catalan cultural figure with the design, construction, and inventive uses of the Grand Café Restaurant he executed for the Universal Exposition of Barcelona. Although slightly altered during several restoration phases, the building today provides a good sense of Domènech's original intentions: architecturally, socially, and even

politically. Among the substantial literature on this building, see Josep M. Martorell, "El Café-Restaurante de la Exposición Internacional," (with English translation) in *Domènech i Montaner Año 2000*, pp. 64–73.

24   For a full listing of Domènech's political posts, see O. Bohigas, "The Life and Works of a Modernista Architect," *Domènech i Montaner Año 2000*, pp. 36, 40; for those posts, cultural and political, held up to 1901, see Lourdes Figueras, "The Hospital de la Santa Creu i Sant Pau: Entre la Función y el Símbolo Modernistas," in *El Hospital de la Santa Creu i Sant Pau, 1401–2001*, pp. 125–26.

25   Each has been designated a UNESCO World Heritage Site. For a chronological list of Domènech's completed major projects, with accompanying thumbnail images, see *Domènech i Montaner Año 2000*, pp. 251–63.

26   See Mireia Freixa, "Domènech i Montaner and Architectural Synthesis," in *Barcelona and Modernity*, pp. 160–163. Clavé did, in truth, have a profound appreciation of opera independent of his organizational activities for the working class. Like other intellectuals in Barcelona, he admired greatly Richard Wagner whose work he introduced to the Iberian Peninsula. In July 1862, he conducted choral and instrumental excerpts from *Tannhäuser* in Barcelona's Teatro del Liceu. Domènech shared the enthusiasm for Wagner and demonstrated it explicitly in the design program for his Palau, where it is explicitly referenced in the large sculptural relief depicting the ride of the Valkyries from Wagner's *Die Walküre* (commissioned from Pau Gargallo, friend of Picasso, Gris, and many others among the avant-garde from Barcelona). See n32 (and Fig. 2.5).

27   See David Mackay, "The Palau de la Música Catalana," in *Domènech i Montaner Año 2000*, p. 74. The essay offers an excellent introduction to the social and architectural history of the Palau, and it has a singularly helpful list of all the collaborators on the building, from locksmiths to majolica workers (pp. 80–82). Further, Mackay documents the "modifications and mutilations," as well as the "repairs and conservation" to the building.

28   As was true for several of Domènech's large projects, funds were periodically in short supply. This was true for the Palau on several occasions between October 1906 and the inauguration of the building on 9 February 1908. Artists and craftsmen were asked to contribute their labor at a discount to further this patriotic enterprise; and the chief architect made representation to wealthy patrons, too. The final costs tallied around 900,000 pesetas, or roughly between $85,000,000 and $100 million today.

29   Exploiting the challenges of an irregular building site animated the design of Plečnik's Zacherlhaus. See below, chapter 3.

30   The use of iron to provide support for arches and openings, and to hold up projecting balconies – most of which cannot be seen from the ground – enabled Domènech to employ a modern technique and material to anchor architectural members that ultimately derive from or invoke Aragon's Mudéjar, Lleida's Romanesque, and other historical styles in Catalonia. As an art historian, Domènech would devote many decades of his life to cataloguing the historical styles that marked Catalonia's architectural richness and diversity.

31   See Mackay, in *Domènech i Montaner Año 2000*, p. 78. Mackay goes on to provide a useful description and analysis of the various spaces of the interior, esp. pp. 76–80.

32   Although the meaning of the imagery remains somewhat unclear, and
to date no original program has been discovered, it is likely that the combination of the outsize bust of Clavé and a comparatively smaller bust
of the great German romantic composer, in the presence of an elaborate
scene from Wagner, represents precisely the ideological and cultural conjunction favored by the Lliga Catalunya and Domènech himself. Wagner
was surely the most celebrated composer in the Catalonia of the time of
the Palau's construction, even as he had been the most noted contemporary composer at the moment that Clavé created the Orfeó. Indeed, ever
since Wagner's 1862 visit to Barcelona (and especially after he conducted
Lohengrin there a decade later), the German composer exerted a profound
influence on Catalan architects (including Puig) and writers, perhaps even
surpassing the impact he exerted on local composers.

33   The Palace contains a number of secondary rooms, rehearsal rooms,
and spaces for the administration. Each is worthy of analysis and discussion. The same is true regarding the building's furnishings. Domènech
played a role in the design, commissioning, and placement of all.

34   The literature on the hospitals is extensive. However, the two essential texts
are the monograph, *El Hospital de la Santa Creu i Sant Pau, 1401–2001,* (with
a series of penetrating essays in Spanish with English summaries, coordinated by Lourdes Figueras and Maria Manadé, and a useful bibliography on
p. 271), (Madrid: Lunwerg Editores, 2001); and the essay by Oriol Bohigas,
"Hospital de Sant Pau," in *Domènech i Montaner Año 2000,"* pp. 86–101.

35   See Lourdes Figueras, "The Hospital de la Santa Creu i Sant Pau: Between the Modernista Function and Symbol," in *El Hospital de la Santa
Creu i Sant Pau, 1401–2001,* p. 245. Figueras identifies the Institut Mental
Pere Mata as "Un primer ejemplo de novedad constructiva aplicada a la
ciencia médica, tanto por su distribución urbana, como por su singular
presencia artística." Ibid., p. 125.

36   See Leopoldo Gil i Nebot, "The Legacy of Paul Gil i Serra," in *El
Hospital...1401–2001,* pp. 236ff., for a detailed description, with extensive
citations of the original French document in which the testator set out a
program of extensive and precise specifications.

The amount of money was substantial and could easily have funded a
1,000-bed facility along with research buildings, and staff costs. By April
1911 the entirety of Gil's legacy for the hospital had been spent (See Oriol
Bohigas, "Hospital de Sant Pau," p. 87).

37   The Eixample, a gridded program with ample opportunity for property
developers is populated with numerous architectural examples of *modernisme* by Gaudí, Puig, and Domènech himself. The hospital complex area
is the rough equivalent of 9 blocks of Cerdà's urban scheme. See Bohigas,
"Hospital de Sant Pau," p. 87.

38   It is important to recognize that the fully mature *modernisme* exam-
pled in Domènech's hospital complex was continued at least until 1912,
when the architect's engagement began to lessen. As a result, the conventional identification of the "end" of *modernisme* and its succession by
noucentisme should be revised. By 1914, Domènech's son, Pere Domènech i
Roura, assumed principle responsibility for the continuation of the works,
although with far simpler designs and more in harmony with the prevailing aesthetics of *noucentisme.*

39   Due to the complicated and necessary changes to the building program coincident with the combination of the two hospitals in a single physical "campus" in la Sarrià, the following discussion treats the initial design and building phases under Domènech's supervision as a single entity. For a detailed examination of all aspects of the hospitals' history, see the essays by Manuel Riu i Rui, Natividad Castejón Domènech, and Josep Danon i Bretos on Santa Creu's medieval and later phases; Anna M. Carmona Cornet's essay on the pharmacy of Santa Creu, and especially those by Vincenç Villatoro, Lourdes Figueras, Àlvar Net i Castel and Paloma Sánchez and Esther Sarrà in *El Hospital de la Santa Creu i Sant Pau 1401–2001*.
   In principle, Domènech was to be responsible for the design of 48 pavilions once the integration of the two hospitals on a single site was fully realized; however, the latter 36 (officially assigned to the Hospital of the Santa Creu) were not completed according to Domènech's original ideas due to the architect's death during the course of the project, due to the lack of funds, and due to the shift in taste of the various succeeding supervising commissions.

40   From the "proceedings of the *Molt Il.lustre Adminstració*, Historical Archive of the Hospital de la Santa Creu i Sant Pau," as cited by Figueras, "The Hospital de la Santa Creu i Sant Pau: Between the Modernista Function and the Symbol," in *El Hospital de la Santa Creu i Sant Pau 1401–2001*, p. 246.

41   See Paloma Sánchez and Esther Sarrà, "El Eco de la Construcción del Hospital de Sant Pau en la Prensa Satírica de la Ciudad. Una Curiosa Anécdota," in *El Hospital de la Santa Creu i Sant Pau 1401–2001*, pp. 195–204.

42   The Catalan vaulting is perhaps best known today as the Guastavino tile vault (or Tile Arch System) as a result of its introduction to and wide usage in North America by the Valencian architect and builder Rafael Guastavino (1842–1908). See John Ochsendorf, *Guastavino Vaulting: the Art of Structural Tile* (New York: Princeton Architectural Press, 2010).

43   Many of the craftsmen and ironworkers whom Domènech retained for the hospital decoration were also employed for the ornamental and structural work at the Palau de la Música, including the sculptors Pau Gargallo and Francesc Madurell i Torres.

44   Gaudí's use of the *trencadís* process likely had a redemptive purpose, as he may have believed that this was a symbolic way of transfiguring the broken and discarded into a higher, integrated purpose. See Juan José Lahuerta, *Antoni Gaudí, 1852–1926: Architecture, Ideology, and Politics* (Milan: Electa, 1992), p. 113.

45   For a detailed discussion of the "Ventilation and Natural Illumination" and of the "Artificial Ventilation and Heating," see *El Hospital de la Santa Creu i Sant Pau 1401–2001*, pp. 243–44.

46   Due to periodic financial exigencies, the hospitals were not completed until 1930, although many of the post-1914 buildings depart considerably from Domènech's plans. Adjacent to the campus a new hospital, bearing no relationship to that of the *modernista* architect, has since June 2009 taken over the principal medical responsibilities of the former one.

47   Domènech was in these same years working on the Mausoleum and Pantheon of King Jaume I (Tarragona), 1906–1908; and making the initial

plans for his own large home the *Casa Domènech* (1908–1910) and that of the *Casa Fuster* (1908–1910), in addition to continuing his work on at least a half-dozen further projects that he had initiated several years earlier.

48   There is a substantial bibliography on the architect. For English readers, the most accessible monograph is Lluís Permanyet, *Josep Puig i Cadafalch* (Barcelona: Ediciones Polígrafa, 2001).

49   J. Puig y Cadafalch, "Don Luis Domènech y Montaner," *Hispania*, vol. IV, no 93, 1902, pp. 540–59.

50   In 1901, upon the mansion's completion, the city conferred upon the design a municipal prize for cultural accomplishment. It is not unlikely that Domènech, who was in office at the time, played a role, although I have yet to confirm this. Also worth noting is the building immediately adjacent, the *Casa Batlló*, which Gaudí would substantially remodel between 1904 and 1906.

51   Like Domènech, Puig was a student of the Catalonian Romanesque his entire life. He described it in *La Renaixença* (11 June 1887, p. 870) as "the sister to our Catalan language" (as cited in Rohrer, *Artistic Regionalism*, p. 122). His own architecture was described in the same periodical (in "Notas artísticas" of 27 June 1897, p. 1132) as building that "spoke modern Catalan – a Catalan which, nevertheless, retained the words of past times, varying only the spelling and syntax." Cited in Rohrer, *Artistic Regionalism*, p. 124.

52   One might mention the *modernista* masters in wrought-iron, Ballarí; in stained glass, Antoni Rigalt; and in stone sculpture, Eusebi Arnau.

53   In 1891 in the pages of *La Veu de Catalunya*, Puig outlined his concept of "artistic regionalism." Rohrer, *Artistic Regionalism*, defines this politicized cultural viewpoint as an attempt "to incorporate a rising Catalanista consciousness and a sense of national [even racial] Catalan character" (p. 104).

54   The process of establishing a commonwealth was initiated as early as 1911. The Spanish king signed the law granting the four Catalonian provinces the legal authority to function as a commonwealth under the crown on 18 December 1913.

55   The Mancomunitat succeeded in establishing a set of cultural and scientific institutions through which to give greater prestige to the Catalan language and culture. Among the most prominent and lasting were the Institut d'Estudis Catalans (Institute of Catalan Studies) and the Biblioteca de Catalunya (Library of Catalonia).

56   The Mancomunitat was dissolved and outlawed under Miguel Primo de Rivera's dictatorship on 20 March 1925.

57   Finally, many of the figures who had been active as *modernistas* continued their architectural practice as *noucentistas*, though in a less high key. Puig, for instance, designed the consummately *noucentisme Casa Joan Pich i Pon* (1921) for the Plaça de Catalunya, just a short distance from his archetypically *modernista Casa Antoni Amatller* (1900). Each building entailed a fundamental renovation of an existing structure to accommodate both living and commercial or office spaces. But through the dramatically differing treatments of the arrangement of spaces, decorative programs, and historical references (gothic and Mudéjar for the earlier building versus Louis Sullivan's 1890 large structures in Chicago for the latter), one can readily appreciate the shift in taste and even ideological purpose.

An even more classicizing example of Puig's work would be his *Casa Lluís Guarro* (1923) erected in Barcelona's Ciutat Vella (Old Town) district. This building also combines offices and dwellings. However, the architect's employment of a classical portico of ionic columns, swags of fruit and garlands, and six classical vases above the cornice (with its dentils) attests to the *noucentisme* popularity of ancient Roman and Greek references for a modern structure.

Joan Pich i Pon (1878–1937), a powerful member of the Radical Republican Party, was politically opposed to Puig and his party. However, both became friendly as councilors within the Barcelona city government, which Pich entered in 1905. Both figures remained politically engaged, through the 1910s, with Pich assuming the presidency of the Cámara de la Propiedad Urbana [Chamber for Urban Property] in 1919, while all the while designing *noucentista* buildings.

3 Jože Plečnik, an Idiosyncratic Slovenian Modernist

In 1989 an essay was published with the provocative title, "A Slavic Gaudi? A Few Remarks about Jože Plečnik."[1] Although the parallels between the Catalan and the Slovenian architects are notable, especially the figures' abiding Catholicism and belief in architecture as an almost sacred mission through which to advance nationalist objectives,[2] a more productive analogy may be adduced with Domènech i Montaner and his circle of *modernistas*. For both the Catalan politician-architects and the Slovenian designer allied themselves with causes that twinned a conservative ideology with a progressive and highly individualized aesthetics through which to assert a distinctive national identity.[3] Moreover, each was engaged with the full range of design, coupling building and decoration, in a concerted campaign to regenerate a (highly selective) past into a usable and meaningful present. This was frequently realized through a close collaboration with politics and politicians.

Plečnik, like Domènech, has occupied a peculiar place in the scholarly (and in recent years, in the popular) historiography, mostly because neither figure conforms to conventional expectations for a modern(ist) architect. Their particular aesthetic progressivism departed essentially from the paradigmatic model of rationalism, internationalism, and anti-historicism that remains the legacy of the idealistic pioneers of classical modern design and landscape architecture.[4] Domènech and Plečnik were inspired both by advanced industrial aesthetics and by the appeal of antiquity, by the possibilities of new building techniques and by age-old methods of construction, by international standards of democratic progress and by chauvinist Catalan or Slavist aspirations. Although the material results of these shared perspectives and practices may be comparable in terms of imaginative stylistic solutions, it is through delving into their motivations and strategies that meaningful parallels might be most suggestively adduced.

Soon after moving to Vienna in 1892, Plečnik studied with and worked for Otto Wagner (1841–1918), first in the Vienna Academy (Akademie der Bildenden Künste) and later in the Austrian's cosmopolitan studio.[5] It was there that the young architect from Ljubljana (then officially known as Laibach) developed a heightened Slavic, and distinctively Slovene, consciousness. Beginning in his student days, he thus committed himself to a lifelong task of developing and consolidating both a generalized (West) Slavic and a particularized Slovenian and South Slavic culture. As we shall see, these efforts were singularly enriched by the classical strain in his formation, promoted in no small measure by his experiences in Italy (1899) as a winner of the Prix de Rome (1898) for his diploma work at the Vienna Academy.[6] However, one must note that Plečnik would revise his attitudes toward Mediterranean antiquity throughout his career,[7] a process that finds an echo in Domènech's selective embrace and reworking of earlier models. Both figures would reject an explicit and archaeologically verifiable classicism (especially Roman art forms and proportions, many of which would be seized upon by the Catalan *noucentisme* artists of the 1910s and 1920s) in favor of a creative "variant" of the past: the Romanesque for the Catalan and the Etruscan for the Slovene, as will be discussed.

Further, as did Domènech (and Puig) in Barcelona, so too did Plečnik in Vienna find generous and supportive patrons among the industrial class. From the very start of the Slovene's career while working within Otto Wagner's orbit, Plečnik capitalized on the older architect's connections among the Austro-Hungarian industrial magnates. Early in 1900, Wagner organized a competition for the important commission let for the Zacherlhaus, the city mansion of offices and dwellings for the wealthy insecticide manufacturer Johann Evangelist Zacherl.[8] At least five assistants from the senior architect's studio or from among his closest young affiliates entered the competition. It was ultimately won by the 28-year-old Plečnik, who had proposed a business partnership with Otto Wagner, Jr.[9] Yet between the designation of the competition winner and the commencement of building, almost three years passed. During this time, Plečnik refined his plans and capitalized on the opportunity to mull over how he might invigorate antique sources for contemporary usage, while steering clear of the contemporary fashions that the young architect deemed transitory and superficial (Figure 3.1).[10]

It is in the upper stories of the Zacherlhaus that one may experience some of Plečnik's most extraordinary innovations. Here, one encounters a decorative cornice of elongated, overlapping granite wedges.[11] These cuneate elements have only the most distant relationship to classical forms, recalling vaguely the imbricated patterning found on

Figure 3.1 Jože Plečnik, *Zacherlhaus*, (1903–1905), Vienna, Jože Plečnik?, original photograph, ca. 1906.
Source: Courtesy of the Plečnik House, Museum and Galleries of Ljubljana.

a classical column torus, for instance. Beneath this impressive cornice decoration, and "bending" beneath the weight from supporting two superposed flat rectangular capitals, is a staggered parade of cast stoneware Atlantids executed by Franz Metzner (1870–1919).[12] Each of these semi-nude musclemen is rendered with an anatomical abstraction that shares little with contemporary Viennese fashion for the elongated and lean. Nor do the figures summon up classical standards of masculine potency. Rather, the rippling rib cages, the brawny hip sinews, the ropey arms, and strapping thighs describe beings equally alien from Max Klinger's monumental semi-nude *Beethoven* (1902, displayed in the Vienna Secession in the same year) as they are from Richard Luksch's 1904 lithesome glazed sculptural panels for the celebrated modern Puckersdorf Sanitarium.[13] The only evident "classical regularity" is Plečnik's rhythmic placement of them around the building in the interstices between the convex windows.[14]

Although granite panels were stipulated by Zacherl himself,[15] their ingenious fastening to a brick supporting wall attests to Plečnik's engineering acumen and technological inventiveness.[16] Likewise, the

Figure 3.2 Jože Plečnik, *Zacherlhaus*, (1903–1905), Vienna, Jože Plečnik?, original photograph, ca. 1906.
Source: Courtesy of the Plečnik House, Museum and Galleries of Ljubljana.

attachment of the vertical ribbing to the exterior is as intelligently re-
solved structurally as it is creatively asserted visually, referring to, but
not emulating, classicizing pilasters. The twinning of imaginative engineering and aesthetic solutions is a foundation of Plečnik's practice.
Moreover, it is one that roots him in the modern respect for technology while freeing him to depart from tradition's stylistic limitations.
Through this cogent conjunction, he remade orthodox building processes and constraining design conventions (or popular fashions) to fit
contemporary requirements. This is as evident on the Zacherlhaus's
complicated exterior as it is a compelling component of the building's
interior.

The awkward site,[17] just meters from Vienna's St. Stephens Cathedral, affected the disposition of internal spaces and, indirectly, the
decorative program. The ovoid staircase, the rectilinear vestibule at
the end of long entrance hallway faced with black marble, and the sequence of floor plans of the various stories were collectively an imaginative response to the demands of the irregular urban plot and
the commercial requirements of the client. For the ground floor vestibule and the ascending staircase, Plečnik's played with the contrast
between light and darkness. This dramatic interplay of chiaroscuro
shaped not only his orchestration of sunlight (today enhanced by artificial light in the vestibule fronting the porter's cabinet) and its fall
on wood-paneled surfaces, but also influenced his stark use of stone
columns without bases or capitals, as well as his creation of a coffered
ceiling that echoed the decorated grids embedded in the floor, most
clearly expressed in the vestibule. All derived from the need to com-
pensate for the peculiarities of the building's position on the redefined
streetscape mandated by the city. But perhaps the most captivating
design features on this interior ascent from shadow to light are the extraordinary and extravagant candelabra that adorn the landings. Each
of these imaginative lighting creations establishes a decorative dia-
logue with the cast figural ornamentation – steers, fish, equine heads,
and cupids – that is contained in the railings, as well as with the fanci-
ful door handles, among the array of ingenious solutions to quotidian
necessities. Plečnik's design resourcefulness extends from the exterior
cornice to interior door handles thus creating a totalizing work that
addresses one visually and haptically. In this, his first independent
architectural project, the architect asserted an idiosyncratic expression that would characterize his extensive international career, and
one that would also consistently engender intensive debate.[18] Moreover, his novel form of aesthetic modernism would, project by project,
be enriched by a decidedly conservative nationalism (and profound
religiosity) (Figures 3.3 and 3.4).

Figure 3.3 Jože Plečnik, *Zacherlhaus*, (1903–1905), Vienna.
Source: Photograph courtesy of Dr. Damjan Prelovšek.

Figure 3.4 Jože Plečnik, *Zacherlhaus*, (1903–1905), Vienna.
Source: Photograph courtesy of Dr. Damjan Prelovšek.

In a telling historical conjunction, Plečnik's Vienna Zacherlhaus is chronologically parallel to Domènech's work on Barcelona's Palau de la Música Catalana and the Hospital Sant Pau. Although there is no evidence of Plečnik being cognizant of contemporaneous developments in the Catalonian cultural capital, the Slovene's initial work in the Habsburg metropolis indicates the geographical scope of comparable concerns shaping a modern architecture. Moreover, the Zacherlhaus, when juxtaposed with our awareness of Domènech's achievements, alerts us to Plečnik's ever developing integration of inventive design and conservative ideology.

Plečnik's combination of ideological reactionism and progressive aesthetics has long been productively appraised regarding his Prague projects, especially his work on the Prague Castle for President Tomáš Garrigue Masaryk (and his daughter Alice) and in his design for the Church of the Most Sacred Heart of Our Lord (1929–1932).[19] In addition, his numerous buildings for his native city of Ljubljana (Laibach) have also been assessed from this perspective. Many of the scholarly studies of individual works have addressed forthrightly the profound role that Plečnik's abiding Catholicism and ultramontane politics played in the generation of the design program and the orchestration of the ornamentation. Less considered has been Plečnik's ideologically inspired programs for the preservation (and adaptation) of Laibach's Roman wall and for Ljubljana's extensive riverine works.[20] In these projects, more emphatically and more imaginatively than others perhaps, the architect sought to manifest both a Slovene aboriginal spirit and a singular Slavic identity within a modernizing urban setting.

Plečnik had initiated his ventures into the landscape with his redesign of the extensive gardens surrounding the historic Prague Castle (*Pražský hrad*), beginning in 1920. The half-kilometer of southern gardens, the first focus for the Slovene, was a showplace for his creativity as both a progressive landscape designer and an architect of decisively "retrospective" vision. It was a laboratory in which to experiment with new forms and innovative conceptions through which to educate the Czechs to the nobility of their heritage while proselytizing for a modern morality. Thus, the sequence of gardens on the south side of the Castle – the Paradise and On Rampart Gardens, as well as the original array of staircases, ramps, bastions, stone bowls, vases, pyramids, tables, mosaic floors, and columns that ornament and complete them – was as much an idealized as a literal landscape. It was a cultivated space in which Central European history was encompassed and modern political philosophy grounded. The ideas he realized in these extensive gardens constitute the architect's first sustained foray into park planning and landscape philosophy. Plečnik's inspired melding of morality and garden design, history and landscape aesthetics, provided him with the philosophical grounds and aesthetic strategies that he would refine and implement in his native land.

By the mid-1930s, the generalized (western) Slavist superpatriotism to which Plečnik and his patrons in Prague had subscribed was eclipsed by a much more particularist and virulent Czechoslovak (and anti-German) nationalism. The atmosphere it established throughout Bohemia and Moravia, and in Prague specifically, discouraged Plečnik from continuing his work there. Yielding to the stridency of Czech chauvinism, Plečnik resigned as Castle Architect in 1935 and shifted his principal focus onto his native soil.

What he learned from his work for Prague's principal castle garden, he endeavored to elaborate in Slovenia, though with one profound difference. Whereas Plečnik was charged by President Masaryk to create a symbolic seat of government worthy of a new state proud of its freedom from centuries of imperial domination, his task in Slovenia was to affirm continuities with past regimes – both actual and imagined. Whereas the commission in Prague was to adapt the past to fit the present; the challenge in Ljubljana was to fit the present into an imagined past. Here, he implemented a redemptive form of reaction by countering contemporary political currents in the Kingdom of the Serbs, Croats, and Slovenes with an archaizing architectural focus. In both Prague and Ljubljana, Plečnik would become an inventive mediator of history.

Despite the different ideologies of his projects in the two Slavic centers,[21] Plečnik drew upon his Czech experience to effect in Ljubljana a triumphal program through which the "traces of the past stand out sharply, using monuments in their capacity as urban marks of orientation and turning them into points of support for collective memory."[22] By so doing, as we shall see, Plečnik sought to transform his native city into a worthy capital for a modern Slovene nation. In short, the generalized Slavic consciousness that he evinced in Prague blossomed into a particularized Slovenian self-awareness. It was this ethnic identity that would determine his original engagement with both an ideated past and a projected future; it would serve, moreover, as the basis for his ingenious designs for a modern Ljubljana.

From his student days, Plečnik believed firmly in the Slavs' civilizing mission for Europe. Holding that we Slavic "artists … are God's elect," he went on to claim "that we are not artists [only] in order to make works of art – but that … we bring ourselves in the search for the beautiful and good – possibly close to God – to the understanding of justice, and make good people – good righteous men as perfect as possible...."[23] The emphasis on the moral dimension of Slavic creativity was easily transfigured by the artist into a religious one, as Plečnik conjoined his abiding adherence to the Catholic faith with a commitment to elevating the spiritual life of his countrymen – primarily through the agency of architecture and landscape design. In this regard Plečnik's Catholicism must be understood as a decisive component of his nationalism; for by fulfilling his numerous commissions for the Church in his homeland, he understood himself as promoting the ethnic identity of the overwhelmingly Catholic Slovenes. In Plečnik's mind, there was a coincidence of the universalist claims of the church and the totalizing aspirations of architecture: each was perceived as transcendent, monumental, and transformative and thereby revelatory of the highest spirit of mankind and nation.[24] Thus Plečnik's faith in the timeless relevance of the church and its teachings went hand in hand with his belief in the authority of architecture to make visible and consequent for a contemporary audience the experience of spirituality. At the most profound level, Plečnik believed in the power of modern architecture to effect salvation – for the individual, for the Slavic race, and for Slovenia.

Like others of his time, and especially among those comprising and supporting the Catalan *Renaixença* and its successive *modernisme*, Plečnik looked to history to identify an ethnic lineage upon which a modern national state might be constructed. Despite his recognition of affinity with and admiration for his fellow Slavs, most notably the Czechs, the architect posited a unique derivation for the Slovenes. Postulating on little concrete evidence that the original inhabitants of central Italy were likely Slavic tribes, he traced to Etruria the origin of the Slovene people. Believing uncritically in a Tuscan pedigree for his compatriots, Plečnik found it fitting to revive and adapt elemental Italian forms – Tuscan columns, door jambs, and tumuli, for example – as a legitimate expression of the "national" architectural idiom. Rejecting the readily accessible Slovenian decorative arts and surviving folk art as sources for a native idiom – and therefore departing from the normative practices of his contemporaries in Slavic Poland, Russia, and elsewhere in the region – the architect turned instead to ancient Etruria as a manifestation "of unspoilt ancient Slovene national art, from which contemporary architecture should draw its inspiration."[25] An Etruscan vocabulary of forms – as well as references to Etrurian spirituality and reliance on ritual – would confer a quasi-classical monumentality commensurate to the ethnic derivation Plečnik hypothesized for his people.

Plečnik's world view was more eclectic than systematic; he borrowed freely from a wide range (and all too frequent misreading) of religious thinkers, historians, and architectural theoreticians. Among the last, the figure who exercised the dominant influence over his architectural perspective (and that of Domènech's too in these same years) was Gottfried Semper (1803–1879), whose arguments in favor of "variety," especially of antique forms, the Slovene would embrace as the foundation of his own aesthetic vocabulary, as was evident in the Zacherlhaus, which he designed while still affiliated with the Habsburg master Semperian, Otto Wagner.[26] What motivated Plečnik was likely the desire to root historically his conservative devotionalism and to justify it with an emotionally charged iconographic program. By means of such a roughly conceived ideology, he desired to counter the ever-growing reliance on the transnational "utilitarianism, typology and standardization [that] are the death of any art,"[27] and the foundation of the modernism advanced in his era by progressive architects and artists throughout Europe. By contrast, Plečnik's world view and practice were informed not by a single style but rather were motivated by an overall architectural expression, one that might advance his unique vision for his Slavic brethren. By drawing upon architectural history, national mythologies, and innovative technological processes, he intended to return architectural design to its originary basis and to provide his native land with a vocabulary of form proportional to his aspirations for it. To effect such an ambitious transformation, Plečnik was favored by a singular conjunction of fortuitous circumstances and natural talent.

Material and political conditions in Ljubljana were ripe for Plečnik just when he was most prepared to take fullest advantage of them. The end of World War I witnessed the creation of the Kingdom of the Serbs, Croats, and Slovenes with Ljubljana designated as the capital city of the Slovenian component of the newly created modern nation of the south Slavs. The local elite, with the encouragement of the royal government in Belgrade, was thus finally in a position to realize the national ambition of making Ljubljana worthy of its status as a capital city. The Yugoslav kingdom passed a building law in 1931 through which the director of Ljubljana's Municipal Building Department was granted unusually free reign to award contacts and implement projects. Hence Matko Prelovšek (1876–1955), the director of the department between 1914 and 1937, was able to vest Plečnik with public commissions of an unprecedented number and scale.[28] These included plans for the capital's green spaces – and the landscape structures designed for them – through which the architect would realize his unconventional modern vision. By considering Plečnik's approach to Ljubljana's Roman wall and his treatment of the banks of the city's Ljubljanica River, we can best perceive his ideologically charged aestheticization of the landscape. But before turning to these pivotal projects that engaged the architect's attention and were ultimately realized with the support of civic authorities, it is worthwhile to note what Plečnik chose not to embrace.

In contrast to most modern architects of large vision, Plečnik rarely worked on apartment buildings and was never interested in public housing projects, neither in Ljubljana nor in Prague. He preferred instead to focus his energies on representative projects, from the most modest to the grandest sale. It is likely that his reluctance to undertake multi-dwelling housing, especially that intended to accommodate workers, was due to his politically conservative belief in the social importance of privilege. He often proclaimed that people of noble mind should serve as an example to those less fortunate. With such a conservative outlook, it is not surprising that he unsympathetically viewed functionalism's belief in modern architecture's mission of "social engineering." Akin to conservative philosophers of his age, whose writings he likely had not read, the architect privileged "natural rights" and a mostly imagined past. These were the keys to unlocking a suppressed "spirit" (of variously Catholicism, Slavicism, and Slovenianism) through which a true and timeless community might be established. For Plečnik architecture, rather than progressive politics, was the means best suited to consolidate and serve modern national communities.[29]

Plečnik held nature (φύσις) to be sacred. He believed that it provided an ideal model, philosophically and historically, for modern man to emulate. His faith in the contemporary value of nature was a conscious attempt to align himself with the philosophy of classical antiquity and, thereby, to make the past an essential part of the present. Although Plečnik's inventive variants on and innovative contextualization of the column, pyramid, and obelisk would ultimately serve as his principal architectural instruments to bring antique forms into current usage, nature – in terms of landscaping – constituted his philosophical strategy: green spaces possess an inherent therapeutic and social value. To revive the citizen's spirit, restore his energies, and remind him of (idealized) democratic values, Plečnik had planted a variety of trees and bushes throughout the central districts of Ljubljana. Along the capital's streets, he diverted sidewalks and pedestrian pathways to allow for the "natural" growth of the countless trees and shrubs he had planted,[30] and thereby hoped to prompt an inspiring encounter with nature's greenery. In Plečnik's theory, greenery would remind urban man of his connection to nature and would soften the harshness and relentless tempo of contemporary city life. But most important of all, a "greened" landscape would be an effective means for the architect to orchestrate one's passage through space and time. And nowhere was this more ingeniously realized than in his strategy for the surviving fragment of the city's Roman wall. Here, one encounters most dramatically the twinned pillars of Plečnik's world view: nature and history combining to shape the modern citizen.

Ljubljana had been founded by the emperor Augustus in 34 B.C. as a Roman colony under the ancient name of Emona (or Aemona). An extensive remnant of the south wall fortification (14–15 C.E.) had been preserved into the 20th century as a reminder of the city's classical past.[31] Behind the wall, on the opposite side of Mirje Street, Plečnik gathered many of the stone fragments from tumbled columns, fallen archivolts, and broken ornaments into a lapidarium, which he treated as if it were one of the many burial chambers that had impressed the architect on his study trip to Rome and its Appian Way (1899). But Plečnik was interested in more than the architectural record. As was the case with his work for Prague, so too in Ljubljana did he desire to reinforce the spiritual and hereditary bonds between the present Slavic inhabitants and the distant past. In the case of the Slovenian capital, these ancestors were the original Roman settlers. To effect this linkage, he needed to do more than merely safeguard the archaeological fragments; he had to transform them into a modern demonstration of historical consequence. Between 1934 and 1937, Plečnik rebuilt the wall and studded its top with a series of pyramids. These pyramids, both surmounting the wall and sometimes implanting themselves firmly on the ground emulate his use of this form for the southern gardens of the Prague Castle, just as they were intended to recall the Pyramid of Cestius (Augustan, c. 18–12 BCE), and thereby reinforce the connection to ancient greatness, one of Plečnik's objectives. However, the triangular forms, occasionally with portals cut through their bases, and with interior chambers, were also intended to evoke the tumuli of Etruria. This evocation at the Roman wall of ancient Etrusco-Italic burial structures was of signal significance to Plečnik, who endeavored to fabricate architecturally an imagined Etruscan genealogy for his compatriots (Figure 3.5).[32]

To give contemporary life to these exalted antique forms, the architect staggered the pyramids rhythmically both atop and alongside the wall, creating along the longitudinal axis an impressive visual syncopation that revealed itself almost cinematographically as the

Figure 3.5 Jože Plečnik, reworking of the Roman Wall, (1934–1937), Ljubljana.
Source: Photograph courtesy of Julia Frane.

pedestrian proceeded along the street. Moreover, Plečnik intended the pyramidal surfaces to be covered with greenery, allowing thereby natural grasses, which he preferred to brightly colored flowers or exotic plants, to vitalize the geometry. Likewise, the verges to each side of the ancient stone wall were landscaped in long bands of grass, establishing a lively contrast to the gray masonry. Further animation was given to the Emonan fortification ensemble through the planting of a row of poplar trees (no longer extant) by which a play of shadows was to enliven the wall surface and with which the rhythmic arrangement of pyramids would have been vertically reinforced. Thus, the citizen of modern Ljubljana, walking or driving along the street on the way home from the city center, would encounter Plečnik's historical narrative, unfolding cinematically from Etruscan, through Roman, to contemporary time. The carefully constructed consciousness of motion through time and space, one of the defining characteristic of classical modernism,[33] was a prominent feature of Plečnik's landscape designs. Yet, when the architect creatively combined historical reference and contemporaneous movement with nature's greenery, he achieved a synthesis that had few parallels in 20th-century art. Perhaps Plečnik's most perfect realization of this fusion of the old and the new, the manmade and the natural, can be found along the Ljubljanica River, which wends its way through the heart and history of the capital city.

The shallow Ljubljanica had often overrun its banks until, during the 19th and early 20th centuries, the riverbed had been deepened and its course channeled through concrete embankments. The work on regularizing the river, long supported from the Habsburg coffers, was halted during World War I, and not until 1930 were the municipal authorities, benefitting from a special appropriation from the royal Yugoslav treasury, in a financial position to continue the project. Marko Prelovšek, in his capacity as director of the city building department, engaged the keen interest and active participation of Plečnik in a host of (realized) riparian design commissions: bridges, storehouses, markets, sluices, and parks among them. It is the last two mentioned that merit attention here.

Plečnik concentrated his efforts on remaking the embankments, beginning as early as 1931 and not ending until 1945. The park project for the upper reaches of the river, in the city districts of Trnovo and Prule, dates toward the beginning of the project, most likely to the years 1932–1933, a full decade after the architect's first efforts at landscape garden design for Prague. As one first approaches this portion of the embankment, say from Plečnik's Cobbler's Bridge (1931–1932), one is immediately struck by the absence of the very monumentality that the architect had championed as both appropriate to the city's genealogy and essential to his fellow citizens' spiritual health. In lieu of an impressive cascade of steps, a panoply of pyramids (as employed at the Emona wall), a complex "fan" of river spans (as instanced by the Three Bridges, 1929–1932), a sequence of "paraphrased Ionic" lampposts (such as his candelabrum outside the Philharmonic Hall, 1932–1933), or an impressive colonnade (as lines the multi-sectioned market, 1940–1944), here one encounters a soothing succession of low, shallow terraces, which follow the gentle curve of the river. Whereas elsewhere along the river bank it is Plečnik's architectural elements that thrust imposingly upward, within this park-like setting verticality is communicated solely by the stand of weeping willows, which crowns the horizontal rise of the terracing. That Plečnik assigned to nature the highest position is noteworthy. On the one hand, it is fully congruent with his garden practice, as we have seen with his stipulation that greenery cap the Roman wall pyramids. But in a deeper sense, Plečnik wished to bring Ljubljana's citizens into a more direct contact with nature and history; and the riverside park commission afforded him an ideal opportunity (Figure 3.6).

Figure 3.6 Jože Plečnik, riverine terraces along the Ljubljanica River, (ca. 1933–ca. 1939), Ljubljana.
Source: Photo: author.

With gently sloping hedged-lined paths leading down from the high embankments and easily accessible from the surrounding streets, the terraces were particularly inviting for citizens to relax, play, or – as Plečnik presumed – launder clothes. Combining utilitarian functions with relaxation and entertainment would lend the terraces wide appeal. But Plečnik wanted to make them instructional as well. To this end, he banked up the slope as to accommodate a progression of low, elongated stone benches in alignment. In such manner, the landscape architecture calls to mind classical parallels congruent with Ljubljana's past, such as a shallow amphitheater or the flutes of a column laid on its side.[34] The park, then, was to be a place where one literally relaxed, played, bathed (or laundered) in an archaeological reprise of the city's Augustan history. As the citizen sat on or walked along the stone benches of Plečnik's "romanized" terraces, she or he presumably might glance across the regulated river to an opposite wall of soothing herbage and pathways, both camouflaging the concrete embankment that Plečnik designed to evoke the green banks and slow windings described by Virgil in the *Georgics* (Figure 3.7).

Figure 3.7 Jože Plečnik, riverine terraces along the Ljubljanica River, (ca. 1932–ca. 1939), Ljubljana.
Source: Photo: author.

If the architect intended his riverbank park to call to mind Latin pastoral poetry, Plečnik wanted to invoke the masculine authority of Roman engineering in his design for the sluice (1931–1935), which lay at the opposite end of Ljubljana's *flumen*. Of course, the lock was of necessity, engineered to perform utilitarian functions; namely, to maintain a constant water level and to regulate the flow in the urban sections of the Ljubljanica.[35] However, Plečnik aspired to monumentalize the ideological significance of the structure and to employ it to promote a stream of historical associations among his fellow Slovenes.

Rejecting the functionalist denigration of decoration, as well as the hierarchical typology of buildings, Plečnik designed his utilitarian sluice as a major public monument, one that would function on multiple metaphoric and literal levels. At a slight distance from the walkways along the river, one can appreciate the greenery cloaking the inclined banks that the architect had planted with native shrubbery and unshaped trees. This park-like framework, which hid from view the reinforced concrete that supported the embankments, is dramatically intensified when seen from the level of the river itself. The woodland-like greensward is complemented at the street level by a procession of paving and gravel that lead directly to the dressed masonry pylon gate. From here the pedestrian initiates his passage through history and across the water. Progressing through an Egypto-Mesopotamian-style portal, the modern citizen of Ljubljana mounts a shallow flight of stairs and then crosses a bridge supported by the three towering pylons of the sluice itself. Traversing the bridge entails more than motion through space. Plečnik wanted it to be a procession through time, too. Therefore, he supported the slender bridge on monumental hybrid Aeolic capitals adorned with carved heads between flaring volutes. This ingenious architectural "composite" was inspired by the archaeological record at Etruscan Cerveteri, where Plečnik may have been impressed by the Aeolic pilasters from the "Tomb of the Reliefs." Plečnik's "Etruscan" shafts were balanced on the other side of the lock gate by equally monumental fluted "Doric" columns, cut off a few meters above the base so that they might serve as stands for enormous antique caldrons, whose imposing gryphon protomes Plečnik knew from his study of Etruscan tomb art, more likely from the books he consulted than from visits to archaeological sites or museum collections. In his invention of original "classicizing" forms, he harkens back to the ornamental Atlantids he first employed in the Zacherlhaus. With such historical elaboration, the sluice bridge was to function as much more than a utilitarian span over the river; rather, it was to engineer a metaphoric transition through Slovenia's genealogy. By an ingenious application of historical reference to the practical task of water regulation, Plečnik unified along the Ljubljanica his nation's history and nature, its ideology and architecture (Figure 3.8).

With its ideologically charged bridge supported on imaginative architectural combinations, the lock gate marked the final phase in the architect's long engagement with redesigning Ljubljana's water course and its urbane mainstream. By 1945, the year of sluice's completion, the favorable conditions under which Plečnik had worked so creatively for his native city changed decisively. Soon after the conclusion of World War II came the end of the Yugoslav monarchy with its relative social conservatism, which Plečnik had genuinely embraced. Moreover, with the imposition of a Soviet system and the imposition of various forms of socialist realism, Plečnik found himself increasingly out of official favor, though never entirely dismissed. The imaginative combination of conservative Catholicism, idealized historicism, progressive engineering, and inventive aesthetics that Plečnik embodied never garnered the favor of the communist party. The now aged architect was

Figure 3.8 Jože Plečnik, sluice gate on the Ljubljanica River, (1939–1945),
Ljubljana.
Source: Photograph courtesy of Julia Frane.

mostly passed over in the awarding of major public commissions to
build a new classless society. Instead of encouraging the idiosyncratic
blend of modernism and ethnic identity formation that Jože Plečnik
personified, Soviet policies proved by and large unsympathetic to
forms of inventive design that departed from party principles.[36] For
Plečnik and his patrons, who celebrated the past as a valued support
of the present and who promoted a modern expression that affirmed
singularity instead of standardization, an era of conservative creativity and inventive optimism had functionally come to an end.[37]

Notes

1   "A Slavic Gaudi? A Few Remarks about Jože Plečnik," in *Jože Plečnik,
    Architect: 1872–1957*, eds. François Burkhardt, Claude Eveno, and Boris
    Podrecca (Cambridge, MA: The MIT Press, 1989), esp. p. 5.
2   Plečnik, akin to Gaudí, adhered to an extreme Catholic religiosity as
    well as to a steadfast spirituality. This shared sacral devotion shaped their
    political sympathies for conservative, sometime ultramontane, candidates

for office and for specific political parties. Although a practicing Catholic, religiosity played a less pronounced role with Domènech (and for Puig and most *modernistas*) despite the fact that every consequential Catalan architect competed for commissions to build churches, restore monasteries, or to house sacred artifacts. For Domènech, religion was more likely decisive as a cultural marker than as a deeply held private spiritual commitment. In this important respect, he differed in both degree and nature from the architecturally determinant Catholicism of Plečnik and Gaudí.

3   "Plečnik's ethical position, joined with his feelings of national duty and a deep religiosity, form the basis for his irreproachably honest confrontation with the phenomena of historicism and the modern movement." *Jože Plečnik, Architect: 1872–1957*, p. 3.

4   In recent years, scholars of modern art and architectural history – in particular, those who focus on eastern Europe – have begun to challenge as too restrictive and too partial the reliance on "Western" modernism as a useful paradigm for comprehending 20th-century art universally. Instead of relying predominantly on "transnational" styles as the most telling index of progressive art, scholars are attending increasingly to the decisive role played by local traditions, expectations, and audiences in the development and expression of a modern art. Just such a contextual perspective, as for example provided by Damjan Prelovšek, *Jože Plečnik, 1872–1957, Architectura Perennis* (New Haven, CT: Yale University Press, 1997), would disclose what he calls, rightly, "asymptomatic" aspects of Plečnik's modernism. Further, the last decade of published scholarship on the history of modern architecture reveals a searching reassessment of the meanings and purposes of "modernist" paradigms as originally established by Walter Gropius, J. J. P. Oud, Le Corbusier, and other fathers of functionalism. See Chap. 1, n1.

5   The scholarly bibliography on Plečnik is substantial. Most recent studies remain indebted to the pioneering research and extensive publications by Damjan Prelovšek. His *Jože Plečnik, 1872–1957, Architectura Perennis* remains a touchstone. Equally important is Peter Krečič, *Plečnik: The Complete Works* (New York: Whitney Library of Design, 1993) and *Jože Plečnik, Architect: 1872–1957*, eds. François Burkhardt, Claude Eveno, and Boris Podrecca (Cambridge: The MIT Press, 1989). Studies devoted to specific sites and projects of Plečnik's activities are manifold and extend from the multi-authored volume on the architect's works for the Prague Castle [*Josip Plečnik, An Architect of Prague Castle*, Zdeněk Lukeš, Damjan Prelovšek, Miroslav Řepa, Tomáš Valena, eds., (Prague: Prague Castle Administration, 1996) and *Die Prager Burg* (Salzburg: Müry Salzmann Verlag, 2016)] to the landscape architecture for Ljubljana (Mansbach, as in n20 as well as in the discussion below).

6   See Damjan Prelovšek, *Josef Plečnik: Wiener Arbeiten von 1896 bis 1914* (Vienna: Edition Tusch, 1979), especially p. 13, n6 for a quotation by the architect on his desire to become ever more a "Carniolan – a Slovene – in the same way as my parents..." (Ms. 31, undated). See also, Damjan Prelovšek, "Architecte Joze Plečnik (1872–1957)," in *Architecte Joze Plečnik (1872–1957)*, exh. cat., (Brussels: Musées royaux des Beaux-Arts de Belgique, 2008), esp. pp. 17–29.

It is noteworthy that both Domènech and Plečnik were awarded the Prix de Rome, although only the later was able to accept it.

7   Among the many idiosyncratic antique but non-classical references in Plečnik's long career is his design of the Vzajemna Mutual Insurance building in Ljubljana (1928–1930), where the columns have been described by Boris Podrecca as "Minoan" variants [see Podrecca, "Bekleidung Kontra Konstruktion – in Gespräch mit Peter Zacherl," in *Josef Plečnik Zacherlhaus: Geschichte und Architektur eines Wiener Stadthauses* [The Zacherl house by Jože Plečnik], eds. Nikolaus Zacherl, Peter Zacherl, Ulrich Zacherl; with contributions from Kenneth Frampton, Franziska Leeb, Ákos Moravánsky, Boris Podrecca, Damjan Prelovšek, Jindřich Vybiral (Basel: Birkhäuser, 2016), p. 211].

8   J. E. Zacherl was the son of the founder of the company, Johann Zacherl (1814–1888), whose fortune was first established through importing via Tiflis (Georgia) the powdered blossoms of the Pyrethrum plant. By 1870 the company was able to manufacture its insecticide powder from locally sourced products in its magnificent "Persian-style" factory designed by Hugo von Wiedenfeld in Wien-Döbling. In keeping with the origins of the plant from whose blossoms the family fortune flowered, the city-center sales facility (Bauernmarkt 7) was ornamented by a large Secessionist mural depicting above the entrance way a Circassian warrior holding aloft the distinctive bottle of Zacherlin Insect Repellent (artist: Josef Maria Auchentaller).

9   For an analysis and assessment of the competition for the commission, see Damjan Prelovšek, "Der Wettbewerb für das Zacherlhaus," in *Zacherlhaus*, pp. 16–53. For the names of those invited to compete, see Ibid., pp. 19–20.

10   According to Ákos Moravánszky ("Granitgewerke," in *Zacherlhaus*, p. 56), the building "reflects little of the great architectural currents of its time.... [It] can be linked to neither the *Jugendstil* nor the Vienna Secession movements...." This may be equally true of Domènech's work in these same years. The Catalan's ornamental vocabulary is essentially inconsistent with Art Nouveau practices. See above, Chap. 2, n15.

11   Significantly, the extensive use of polished granite on the building's exterior was the choice of the client and not that of the architect (See Moravánszky, Ibid., p. 72 and Prelovšek, "Der Architekt und seine Bauherr" in *Zacherlhaus*, p. 115).

12   The importance of these Atlantids for the architect cannot be underestimated. From the time Plečnik acquired his own house in Ljubljana until his death there, the single photograph adorning his bedroom-cum-private architectural studio was an image of the Zacherlhaus Atlantids, shown here as Figure 3.2. It would have been the focus of his attention whenever he would look up from his work table.

Metzner is perhaps best known for his sculpture adorning the Palais Stocklet in Brussels, designed by Josef Hoffmann. The sculptor had consolidated his international reputation by being awarded the gold medal at the Paris Exposition Universelle of 1900, and was thus an appropriate artist to whom the wealthy manufacturer could let a commission. For his work for the Zacherlhaus, see Damjan Prelovšek, "Der Architekt und sein Bauherr," pp. 118–19. See also, Anthony Alofsin, *Frank Lloyd Wright, The Lost Years, 1910–1922*, (Chicago: University of Chicago Press), pp. 127–32, and Maria Pötzl-Malikova, "Franz Metzner und die Wiener Secession," in *Alte und Moderne Kunst*, vol. 21, nos. 148/149, 1976, pp. 30–39.

13   One might also note the girdle with its emphatic vertical scabbard and fall of drapery from just below the navel to well beneath the knees. The pattern, approved by Plečnik, is once again counter-classical. Of equal sculptural significance is the large bronze figure of the Archangel Michael, for which Plečnik composed figure drawings before giving his program to Ferdinand Andri (1871–1956) for execution. The sculpture was complete by 1905; it was exhibited in the XXX Exhibition of the Vienna Secession in 1908. The style of the work, as well as its eccentric placement on the Wildpretmarkt façade of the Zacherlhaus, are indicative of Plečnik's creative individuality.

14   Alofsin, among others, asserts Metzner's embrace of Assyrian and Egyptian references for the Atlantids and, especially, for the crypt sculptures executed between 1908 and 1913 for the Völkerschlacht monument just outside Leipzig.

15   It is not certain whether Zacherl's keen interest in granite as a building material was purely aesthetic, as Prelovšek and others assert, or whether there may have come into play an ideological commitment. Julius Langbehn (1851–1907), a notably popular right-wing philosopher and art historian, had written in his extremely well known and often quoted (and recently published) nationalist tract, *Rembrandt als Erzieher* (Leipzig: C.L. Hirschfeld, 1890, p. 221) that "[D]ie Griechen hatten eine Kultur von Marmor, die Deutschen sollten eine solche von Granit haben. Der Granit is ein nordischer und germanischer Stein...." [The Greeks had a culture of marble, the Germans should have one of granite. Granite is a northern and German stone.]. It is likely that both patron and architect were aware of the claim, especially as it was echoed by similar assertions elsewhere in Europe. In Baltic Estonia, for instance, gray limestone was proclaimed the "national stone." (See S. A. Mansbach, "Modernist Architecture and Nationalist Aspiration in the Baltic: Two Case Studies," *Journal of the Society of Architectural Historians [JSAH]*, vol. 65, no. 1, March 2006, p. 100 and n32).
For Plečnik the use of such expensive stone would be a comparative rarity, as the architect most often sought economical materials and methods in his architectural, if not in his religious utensils. Zacherl himself opted for the costly granite, just as he did for the black marble used in the walls of the elongated entry hall and in the columns employed in the vestibule, which is situated between the notably long entrance hall and ovoidal staircase.

16   See Podrecca, "Bekleidung," in *Zacherlhaus*, pp. 207–8.

17   For a discussion of the site, made all the more challenging by the passage of new urban planning policies by the Vienna city government, see Prelovšek, "Der Wettbewerb," in *Zacherlhaus*, pp. 28–29.

18   The immediate reception in Vienna to the Zacherlhaus was as controversial as it was extensive. See Prelovšek, "Der Architekt und sein Bauherr," in *Zacherlhaus*, pp. 122–27. Perhaps the most enthusiastic supporter of the building was Peter Altenberg, an associate of Adolf Loos:

> [The Zacherlhaus] is indescribable, the impression of this noble, simple, and yet mysterious palace of the gods, a modern, habitable Valhalla in the midst of a thousand cardboard blocks! As if it has grown out of the soil and its own noble power! Structured like basalt rocks,

its sharp walls. It moved me like tragic, epic poetry. Breaking conventions, prevailing, and devastating with the tremendous power, and heralding a new world order...!

Quoted in Prelovšek, ibid., pp. 124–25

19   Several of the sources cited in the notes to this chapter contain extensive analyses and manifold bibliographical references to the work Plečnik completed in Prague between his arrival in 1911 and his final departure 20 years later (Plečnik initially departed Prague in 1921 to assume a professorship in architecture in Ljubljana).

20   Much of the following discussion is taken from Mansbach, as in Chapter 1, n13, and from Steven A. Mansbach, "Jože Plečnik and the Landscaping of Modern Ljubljana," in *Centropa: A Journal of Central European Architecture and Related Arts*, eds. Steven Mansbach and Joachim Wolschke-Bulmahn, vol. 4, no. 2, May 2004, pp. 110–20.

21   Plečnik's secular work in Prague, especially the garden landscapes, courtyard, and presidential apartments and staircases he designed for the Castle should not be understood as an uncritical affirmation of the democratic world view that President Masaryk had so long promoted. It is more likely that the architect privileged the scope and variety of the creative possibilities that the various Castle commissions offered. It is probable that Plečnik enjoyed the conversations he had with the Czechoslovak president on the history of the Slavic peoples rather than on political systems. Likewise, it is feasible that the architect relished his exchanges with Alice Masaryk on religious topics more than on liberal sociopolitical ones.

22   See Jörg Stabow and Jindřich Vybíral, "Projects for Prague," *Architect of Prague Castle*, p. 432.

23   From an undated letter from Plečnik to Jan Kotěra as cited in Prelovšek, *Jože Plečnik, Architectura Perennis*, p. 13.

24   Plečnik was as committed to Catholic Slovenia (within the framework of the multi-confessional Habsburg Empire and the succeeding two Yugoslavian states) as he had once been to the mostly non-Catholic nation of Masaryk's Czechoslovakia, although for different reasons. It was primarily as a professor and as the Castle [Hrad] Architect that he had achieved renown in Czechoslovakia and not principally as a religious architect, despite the signal success of the Church of the Most Sacred Heart of Our Lord (1929–1932). In Slovenia, by contrast, he would realize a substantial number of churches, the majority outside the capital, and for which he would design ritual artifacts and religious vessels until the end of his life.

25   See Prelovšek, "Ideological Substratum," *Architect of Prague Castle*, p. 99, n7.

26   Plečnik had not been an outstanding student; however, stimulated by his elder brothers, Andrez and Janus, and by his later discussions with Masaryk, he acquainted himself with historical and religious texts. Regarding the history of architecture, he educated himself much more carefully and systematically. For an analysis of the importance of Semper (in particular his *Die vier Elemente der Baukunst* [1815] and *Der Stil in den technischen and tektonischen Künste oder Praktische Asthetik* [1860–1863]) for Plečnik's aesthetic development, see Prelovšek, *Jože Plečnik, Architectura Perennis* and Prelovšek, *Josef Plečnik: Wiener Arbeiten*.

27   Cited in the unpublished manuscript by Vinko Lenarčič, *Spomini na Plečnika* [Recollections of Plečnik], c.1961–1963) as quoted by Prelovšek, *Jože Plečnik, Architectura Perennis*, p. 260.

28   With Director Prelovšek's encouragement, Plečnik prepared the first of several master plans for his native city between 1926 and 1928, setting out his ambitious program for a Slavic metropolis. Although the full scope was never implemented, cardinal civic and religious projects were substantially realized: public squares during the latter half of the 1920s (including the St. James'/Levstikov, Congress, and French Revolution Squares) the University and the National Library from 1936 to 1941; churches and monasteries from the 1920s through the 1950s; bridges, markets, and monuments during the 1930s and 1940s; cultural, commercial, and governmental buildings; villas and private houses, and parks, promenades and public passageways and staircases. See Prelovšek, *Jože Plečnik, Architectura Perennis*, pp. 262–73.

29   See Jörg Stabenow, *Jože Plečnik: Städtebau im Schatten der Moderne* (Braunschweig/Wiesbaden: Vieweg Verlagsgesellschaft, 1996), p. 40.

30   Plečnik preferred not to sculpt trees or contour bushes; rather, he advocated leaving them in the natural state and using them as "natural shapes" (both in his Bohemian and Slovenian commissions). As a result, he favored for Ljubljana trees with distinctive "profiles": birch, poplar, plane, and weeping willows, among other species. Significantly, the architect chose few species that carried classical references from Latin poetry. Hence, there are comparatively few oaks or cypress trees, for instance, in his landscape programs.

31   Although the south wall was the most visible surviving portion of the Roman surrounding stonework, standing to a height of about three meters after its renovation by Walter Schmidt in the 19th century, Plečnik treated at least one additional wall fragment, where the medieval city wall intersects a segment of the original Roman wall, just in front of the National and University Library (Plečnik, 1936–1941). The architect had the Roman portion resurfaced in local cut stone and then allowed it to be covered in greenery. This combination of herbage, local masonry, and remnants of antiquity was, as claimed in the present study, an ideological strategy Plečnik favored.

32   Perhaps nowhere is this more forcefully realized than in the architect's program for the city's principal cemetery of Žale [an old Slavic word for cemetery] (1938–1940). Here, Plečnik advocated funerary monuments based on Etruscan rounded tumuli or pyramidal forms, and often concealing internal chambers under a layer of earth and grass. For an excellent English-language discussion, see Anthony Alofsin, *When Buildings Speak: Architecture as Language in the Habsburg Empire and Its Aftermath, 1867–1933* (Chicago, IL: Chicago University Press, 2006), pp. 243–46.

33   Although thematized variously as "space-time," "vision in motion," or even "a new fourth dimension," the engagement with movement through space and time was the decisive feature for the classical avant-garde in creating a modern art (as well as science and society) during the first three decades of the 20th century. Among the numerous classic texts on this topic, see Sigfried Giedion, *Space, Time and Architecture. The Growth of a New Tradition* (originally the Charles Eliot Norton Lectures for 1938–1939)

(Cambridge, MA: Harvard University Press, c. 1941) regarding architecture and the nature of its modern character; and, especially, the writings of Theo van Doesburg, El Lissitzky, and László Moholy-Nagy, who, along with a host of Russian and Polish figures, may collectively be identified as the originators of the concept as applied to modern art generally. Representative of the nature and authority attributed to space-time is the following citation from Moholy-Nagy (*Vision in Motion* [Chicago, IL: Paul Theobald, 1947], p. 266):

...a new dynamic and kinetic existence freed from the static, fixed framework of the past. Space-time is not only a matter of natural science or of aesthetic and emotional interest. It deeply modifies the character of social ends....

34 Prelovšek (*Jože Plečnik, Architectura Perennis*, p. 292) was the first to associate Plečnik's stone terraces with the flutes of a column.

35 According to Prelovšek (*Jože Plečnik*, ibid.), Plečnik also had the idea to use the sluice to make the river navigable, and consequently planned a landing dock nearby. He also envisioned a small hydroelectric power station to be connected to the sluice. See K. Dobida, "K načrtu zatvornic na Ljubljanici," [On the plan for the lock on the River Ljubljanica], in *Mladika*, 1, 1935.

36 In the decade from the end of World War II, Plečnik received few major public commissions in his native land or in Czechoslovakia. However, in 1952, he was allowed to be awarded an honorary doctorate from Ljubljana University. Moreover, in the year preceding his death in 1957, rather unexpectedly the architect received a commission from the Yugoslav party and national leader, Marshall Tito (1892–1980). Paradoxically, this commission permitted Plečnik to complete his career among Slavs in the same way he began it; namely, by designing a private retreat for the president of the respective republics: the Palace of Lány (and the private apartment in the Castle) for Czechoslovakia's T. G. Masaryk, and a villa on the island of Brioni for Yugoslavia's Josip Broz Tito (prime minister from 1945 to 1953; president from 1953 to 1980).

37 Plečnik's engagement in religious architecture continued until the end of his life. In fact, one might appreciate his designs of the 1950s for church architecture (and the necessary ritual objects – chalices, baptismal fonts, and so forth) as imaginatively striking, even if somewhat "mannered" in their elaborate decoration (See Krečič, *Plečnik: Complete Works*, p. 179). During the last decade of his life, the architect was able to complete several of the projects he had begun years earlier and for which funds were then insufficient (as, for example, in the Church of the Ascension of Christ at Bogojina). However, one should note the rebuilding of the Church of St. Benedict in Zgornje Stranje (1947–1954), whose almost total destruction during World War II afforded Plečnik the chance to design, construct, and furnish a complete church, one that blended folk forms (especially in the southern portico and in many of the balusters) and plebian materials with highly refined ones (as in the colored stone used in the baptistery and the metal employed for the variety of lamps in the nave). For a good introductory analysis see, Maja Avguštin, "Church of St. Benedict," in *The Architect Jože Plečnik: Guide to Monuments*, introduction and photographs by Damjan Prelovšek, ed. Nataša Gorenc (Ljubljana: Institute for the Protection of Cultural Heritage of Slovenia, 2008), pp. 95–100.

4 Reflections on Modernism's Complexity

Jože Plečnik's idiosyncratic modern architecture combined a commitment to modern technologies with a reworking of tradition. Such a concurrence informed his work from his first independent project in Vienna through his noble endeavors in Prague to his prolonged engagement to remake the urban landscape of his native Ljubljana. What united the rich array of his projects was an abiding belief in the power of a modern architectural expression to articulate the national or ethnic character of Slavs generally and of the Slovenes specifically. To realize his nationalist ideology, Plečnik resisted the ideological precepts of High Modernism, which were being forcefully projected in word and concrete by J.J.P. Oud's and Theo van Doesburg's De Stijl, by Walter Gropius's Bauhaus, by the Russian Constructivists with their designs for a "great utopia," and by classical modernists throughout the globe. In the very years when the fundamental faith in rationalism, anti-traditionalism, and transnationalism were being stridently advanced by an ascendant functionalism, Plečnik was demonstrating the potency of a different kind of modernism. His progressivism embraced new technology and engineering processes; but it also affirmed the essential value of historical forms and antique references, and the critical importance of an extensive use of imaginative ornamentation, as the best means to conserve, consolidate, and ultimately to celebrate that which is local, distinctive, and satisfying. His forms of modern architecture necessarily resisted the postulates of High Modernism's socialism: economic, political, and aesthetic. For Plečnik, a truly progressive architecture had to be annealed through conservative values and ethnic affirmation.

This melding of a reactionary ideology with a progressive design practice defined the world view of Plečnik. But a version of it had already been creatively expressed and magnificently realized in Barcelona. Lluís Domènech i Montaner and his *modernista* confederates had also, and with greater effect, understood the essential conjunction of conservative politics and advanced architecture. Whereas Plečnik's political sympathies were often sublimated through his collaboration with patrons and sponsors – a Viennese industrialist, a Czechoslovak president, and a Ljubljana city official, for instance – the Catalans were in an absolutely unique position. They were themselves both the political officials who commissioned major projects while also serving as the architects who carried them out. Hence, *modernisme* took deep root in Catalonia at a decisive period of its cultural and political evolution. Through a distinctive blend of a conservative politics and an ingenious vocabulary of visual and structural design, Domènech, Josep Puig i Cadafalch, and their collaborators became the true architects of Catalan nationalism.

The ethnocentrism of Plečnik and the nationalism of the Catalans exemplify the variety of ideological potential and aesthetic innovation to which a modernizing architecture can lend itself. It befits us to keep these cases in mind as historians and critics continue the worthy effort of recognizing in modernism less a single or uniform "movement" than a complex creative endeavor characterized by diversity, individuality, and idiosyncrasy. The promise of such open-mindedness is an enhanced appreciation of how both an ideologically motivated conservativism and a more familiar liberal aspiration together constituted the foundation for progressive design and advanced aesthetics.

Appendix

Lluís Domènech i Montaner's seminal "En busca de una arquitectura nacional" originally appeared in *La Renaixensa*, 28 February 1878, year VIII, number 4, vol. 1, pp. 149–160. (The Hemeroteca Digital [Digital Newspaper/Periodical Library] of the Biblioteca nacional de España has digitized the journal, much of which is currently available at the following website: http://hemerotecadigital.bne.es/details. vm?q=id:0004204395.) The appendix presented here is the first full English translation. It is the result of the careful joint preparation by José María Naharrro-Calderón, Professor of Iberian Literatures and Cultures at the University of Maryland, and the art historian Àngels Ferret-Ballester. The translation has endeavored to communicate the literary texture of Domènech's complex sentence structure, frequently rebarbative syntax, and often idiosyncratic vocabulary – all the while making it comprehensible for a modern audience. Slight alterations to enhance clarity and readability have been made by the author of the current volume, drawing on both the Catalan original and several Spanish translations.

Looking for a National Architecture

The final word in any conversation about architecture, the capital question of any criticism, turns on one idea: modern national architecture.

And there is no way out of this question, in spite of ourselves, but to ask:

Can we have a true national architecture today? Could we have it in the near future?

The architectural monument, as with the greatest of all human creations, requires the energy of a productive idea, a moral environment through which to live, and ultimately the physical means to shape itself, as well as a more or less perfect and accommodating idea that [might provide an] instrument for an artist's ideas, as well as the moral and physical means for the architectonic form.

Whenever an organizing idea dominates a people, whenever a new civilization breaks out, a new artistic age begins.

The Indian civilization, Brahmanism, with its grandiose religious and cosmological ideas [arose] amidst the natural horizon of the vast plateau of the Himalayas, on a land watered by giant Asian rivers, among the fauna and natural colossus. [These great rivers and Brahmanism have] cut the mountains with a bold chisel, building the [great religious caves of] Mavalipuram, Elephanta, or Ellora.

Despotic monarchy sprang from the mud of the Tigris and the Euphrates, with all of their imposing and majestic grandiosity, their immense palaces [built] over clay thrones on the calcinated flames of Chaldea, Assyria, and Persia, dominating successively and eventually over the whole world.

The theocratic principle and faith in eternal life raised indestructible granite palaces on the banks of the Nile, and the temples of Karnak and Ramesseum, as well as of Deuderah and the island of Philae.

The republican form and the cult of the individual [man] elevated to a semi-god created the Parthenon and the Temple of Theseus.

The political idea, the principle of social order gave life to the Coliseum, to the Column of Trajan, and to the Thermal Baths. Even the fanatic, warmongering, and sensual genius of Islam, once its floodtide was contained and while resting from its victories, [exploited its creative power] over marble columns and on the shadows of a Byzantine temple, braided the sunny Andalusian golden rays as on the Alhambra plaster ribbons and tiles.

Christianity, in its cradle, repurposed thousands of destroyed temples for their ideal [aesthetics], with many attesting to the beauty of their work: San Vitale in Ravenna, San Marco in Venice, and Santa Sophia in Constantinople. And when in the Middle Ages, the oppressed vassal saw the cross as the sign of eternal and secular redemption, then the village's secular schools rose in front of the fortress, in front of the feudal castle, and before the sublime temple of idealism: the Christian cathedral.

Only societies without firm or fixed ideas, fluctuating between today and yesterdays' thought and void of faith in the future, do not write their history in enduring monuments. Their ideas are as transient as the monuments to which they give birth. On moral grounds they are like those desert planes, without a drop of water to temper them, with their transitions from a fiery sun to frosty irradiated nights, where only lower plants may root. The palm tree gently swings its flexible branches at the burning current of the Simoom, the snowy mountain's fir defies inflexibly the icy north wind; however, neither one may resist the alternatives of mornings in July, and a January night in the sweet climate of our regions.

In times of transition, when ideas are fought relentlessly, in the midst of discordant notes from overall passions, it is impossible to imagine the great harmony reflected during eras of true architectonics. If modern civilization were not to be shaped by internal struggle, if the general public could guide artists with its opinion and applause, a new architectural era would undoubtedly arise; and it eventually will, albeit with the slow pace shown by artistic movements. Never before have so many elements come together. The just and insightful ideas initiated by Christianity are transferred from the individual spirit to the one in state regimes, practically in some cases, and in others, as not yet fulfilled aspirations. Formal and personal questions, rather than ideas, produce this continuous struggle where modern society consumes its greatest resources. But the necessities that these ideas lead to in the administration of civil nations, and the creation of buildings that will satisfy them, are admitted by all sorts of thinkers. At the same time, ancient civilizations surrender to us their treasures of knowledge and artistic forms; museums fill themselves with models of profitable teachings; printing quickly disseminates studies carried out as much about the ruins of Babylon, Nineveh, Persepolis, Ellora, Mexico, Thebes, Troy, Athens, and Rome, as for those immense buildings erected in a single day of delirium by the industrial genius [if only] to destroy them the next day; a weak creature's hand assisted by electricity; and chemistry demolishes at its will the gigantic marble mountains; iron burns in the blast furnace in order to be bent and to surrender itself docilely to us through the rolling mill's domination; mechanical science already determines the rudiments of architectonic form; and in the realm of sound, harmonic resolutions reveal the artistic laws of proportions and chromatic harmony; nations finally open their treasures to artists so they may shape on real grounds their ideal concepts. Everything announces the advent of a new era for architecture, but it is necessary to admit that we are still missing a public with good taste and asserted ideas, one to whom the teaching of decorative drawing in schools or the practice of art appreciation would provide a guiding artistic feeling, as [was the case with] the Greeks with their architects at the Athenian agora, and modern artists in their thoughts. Today's architect encounters modern civilization's complicated spectrum of endless artistic and material needs, and with infinite means to solve them. But sometimes due to lack of lack of satisfactory instruction at the time of his formal education, or at times lacking enough talent to apply the acquired knowledge, modern artists feel more dominated by the working materials than dominators, and only after a while which we do not dare to gauge, shall they be able to gather in their creations all the materials that civilization provides from day to day. Only after severing all ties to rancid and ignorant school concerns, and by avoiding the spotlight on an ostentatious imagination, since public opinion will rather appreciate the simplest works, modern architecture, daughter and heiress of all that has past, will rise above them, bejeweled with their treasures as well as with the industrial and scientific ones it has acquired.

But such an architecture will be, like all of its predecessors, the art of a generation; it will represent a civilization but not a region. In other words, under modern society's current conditions, architecture cannot maintain a truly national character. The spirit of a nation itself may modify the general modern type, may set up a school, a gradation, but not a different art with its necessary conditions; that is to say, with its own construction and ornamental systems. The continued expansion of knowledge across borders, the powerful assimilation force of modern instruction, the organizational similarity among people will nullify all the efforts to create a national architecture. Roman art is not Roman because of its place of origins, but due to the fact that it represents Roman civilization. If a new architecture could be created in a nation responding to the needs of the day, it would soon spread out to other civilized countries which profess ideas and possess similar means. It would be a modern but not a national architecture.

It is true that the secular character of a people, its artistic traditions, and climate may profoundly vary the necessities for buildings in [any] two countries, even though they respond to the same order of ideas. These gradations among the same architectural ideas may become visible among people, each different from one another by means of character, climate, and defined traditions. But for the peoples that constitute the current Spanish nation this common gradation for all in modern art will not be possible until the day on which the latter [i.e. modern art] shall constitute itself completely.

What are our common artistic traditions? And our common character? What physical environment should be considered as national?

Neither the same history, nor the same language, equal laws, customs, or inclinations have shaped the diverse Spanish character. The most varied climates, the most diverse lands, in their topography, formation, and nature, constitute the different regions of Spain; it is only natural that these circumstances gave birth to predominant artistic traditions, generally Arabic in the south, Romanesque in the north, Ogival or Gothic, in its popular denomination, in the former lands of the Aragonese Crown and ancient center of Spain, and Renaissance in the cities born from the centralizing power of the Habsburg and Bourbon monarchies.

Starting with these artistic elements, it is difficult to form a more distinctive architectonic unity that is more Spanish than any other nation's, and that is equally pleasing to all of us.

We could have it if Pelagius and Wilfred could be blended into a single figure; if [the Battle of] Roncevaux, the conquest of Seville and the expedition to Greece were to be recognized as a single people's glory; or when the energetic and quiet chant of *Tcheco jaona* and the ballad of the *Count Arnau* could be sung and understood by those who modulate with Southern outbursts of fire and the lassitude of the picturesque *Playera* or the sad *Soledad* melodies, when the matrons of our Catalan farmhouses would learn to tie to their hair a red carnation bouquet, so well suited over a dazzling Andalusian light sun-tanned forehead. Finally, we could form it when the moral and materially solid genius of the Galicians, the valiantly faithful Basques or Navarreses, the active Catalans, and the ingenious Andalusians could come together in one single character.

And all these and many other unifying elements could shine within a national taste and art if, as in civilized Greece, Assyria, or Egypt, a similar climate and identical materials would force artists to adopt specific fundamental forms. But this powerful unifying element does not exist either. The climate of the South is almost as burning as Africa's, and the Cantabrian Sea can very well match some northern European countries.

Geology, and therefore, topography could not be more rugged. A variety of granite and porphyritic eruptions sprout throughout Spain presenting the largest overall broken terrain, and altering the materials laid exposed in each region. It would be a curious but impossible study to carry out here, to compare in detail the nature of Spanish towns with the land that sustains them: for example, Galicia and Asturias, considered the same region morally with their granitic, gneiss, and silurian ground preponderance; the Basque and Navarre provinces with the ancient secondary or tertiary soils on which they stand; Catalonia with its complicated set of geological accidents summarizing the history of the world on a small scale; Aragon and both Castiles with those three large lakes of calm tertiary waters that constitute them, and finally, Andalusia with the white tertiary or alluvial basins still fertilized by the Guadalquivir and the Guadiana [Rivers], between the oldest rough mountains and the metamorphic terrains that provide them with timber for construction and fuel, as well as marble and metals.

Beyond this set of external circumstances, in order to build a national and modern architecture, four tendencies stand out among artists, and even more among critics.

The first and oldest, widespread in Europe at the beginning of the century, is proudly given the name of classical or Greco-Roman. The present generation knows and respects too much Greek art, and the brilliant Roman architectural constructions and dispositions, to admit either such name or simulacra of architecture. The majestic Doric, the elegant Ionic, and the graceful and rich Corinthian columns, round in plan, served as isolated support for their corresponding porticoes, in order for multitudes to circulate under; since they didn't support more than a simple ceiling, and lightly and airily set their base on firm ground. As part of a constructive member wisely arranged in its object, under pseudo-classic architecture, they [the classical order of columns] lost their serious character. Forming sometimes in front of the facades, a sort of bowling castles on top of each other, as irresponsive forms and useless objects for construction, crushing themselves, at times with their own capitals, against Greek good taste; in pilaster form, like temples used as rental homes, balconies, and windows appear, breaking the vertical lines haphazardly. The unstable cylindrical form which the Greeks strove to accentuate and affirm with fluted lines, is often displayed plainly; and the capitals, a masterpiece that they tried without satisfaction to improve a thousand times, dare to bear the bastardly Tuscan form.

The pediment appears in classic temples as the element of a building cover, always aware of its imperfect lower angles, and ensuring an apparent stability through the acroteria; here it presents itself lavished with meagre forms on façade openings, breaking the sloping sides with their moldings in any shape and form against the cornice, and without the palliation that classic taste provided against this defect.... Why repeat what has already been made popular, in full volumes, by Viollet-le-Duc, Boutmy and so many others? This sort of architecture has [already] been completely abandoned everywhere, since it unconsciously destroyed excellent Medieval works, badly copying forms without understanding the classic sentiment; today it is already a corpse, or rather, the repugnant mummy of classical architecture due to its distorted forms and lack of reason for being and living. Nevertheless, it still has some supporters even among those who practiced it before, or who boast being scholars, always complaining about times that have vanished, without amending the present, nor preparing the future.

Another eclectic but respectable school tries to preserve classical traditions by applying them to the buildings to which they give life and adjust to naturally. This school, like the previous one, is not exactly national and is based on a true study of the well-known ancient classical or art of the Middle Ages. This school's central principle is German. For them, a cemetery must be Egyptian or some other style; a museum, Greek; a parliament, Roman; a convent, Byzantine or Romanesque; a church, Gothic; a university, Renaissance; and a theatre, half Roman-half Baroque, and so on, with small variations. It is necessary to declare that this school demonstrates [historical] knowledge, but we don't believe we should support it. The old forms don't adjust to our current needs or construction means; and this school's authors are very frequently required to disregard their attachment to tradition and [architectural] objectives by hiding the modern means they employ (for example, the main beam, the iron column): they can hardly disguise it when they respond to a real necessity worthy of being exposed ... And we would find it sad for the present generation, when evaluated by the next, to be stripped by the latter of all its monuments, without leaving a form of its own.

Finally, two other rationalized tendencies, worthy of appreciation in their origins, are those that attempt to pursue the traditions of the Middle Ages, alas interrupted in architecture by the Renaissance. The first among the two schools prefers the Romanesque and Ogival monuments and consequently the Aragonese school, a homeland tradition so well represented in Catalonia. The second caters to Arabic architecture or its modifications by Muslim masons or *alarifes* imported into Christian society, generally known under the name of "mudéjar," with abundant samples mainly in Toledo. If three or four centuries would not have elapsed from the time that both styles went out of fashion, if we could remain isolated from the European movements, they could constitute two different types of national architecture: one that perhaps could be applied to the south and center of Spain, and another that could be adopted by our nation's easterners. Perhaps both could blend and violently form a third type of architecture; but frankly, based on reasoning and sentiments, this road would not lead to a brilliant era of modern architecture. We studied with enthusiasm for hours and days each of the monuments from both styles in architecturally rich Toledo, and every day as we returned through the misty Tagus to our inn on the Alcázar slope, reflecting upon that day, we gained new admiration for what had been built, but felt disappointed for what laid ahead. One cannot deny the advantage of borrowing from both styles versatile compositions. A single building that springs from these traditions shows it: the new and perfectly composed Vienna arsenal.[1] But on the latter, and any new one with both styles, elements would not be enough to satisfy today's requirements. How would the great hall of a theatre be held up, for example, to the proportions of Arabic and Gothic art where the vertical preponderance is so relevant? How could we obey the highly rational economic and building laws that force us to use iron with mechanically determined new forms? How do we follow norms that in large halls determine the acoustical and optical laws, if we also have to subject them to forms not studied for these objects? We would never reach the bottom if we wanted to indicate all the difficulties that in practice bar and require us to resort to new forms, disguised as Gothic or *Mudéjar*, covered up with four sets of dead leaves from the period, manifesting the poverty of our creativity.

Why not frankly accomplish our mission? Why not prepare, since we can't form it, a new architecture? Let us inspire ourselves in the homeland traditions provided that they don't prevent us from overlooking what we have gained or may acquire.

Let us admit and be guided in architecture by the necessary teaching principles from past ages. Let us attach decorative forms to the construction as in classical times; let us be mesmerized in Eastern architectures by their imposing majesty through the predominance of horizontal lines and large, smooth or slightly worked up surfaces, in contrast with the richly decorated grandiose ornamental motifs formed by Assyrian or Persian sphinxes; let us remember the principle of solidity in Egyptian firm lines; let us try to acquire the treasure of good taste from Greek temples; let us study the secrets of Roman greatness in composition [*distribuciones*] and construction, or material idealization in the Christian temple, as well as the system of multiple forms of ornamentation, all connected to one another, that provides clarity and order at different distances as in Arabic decoration; let us finally learn the elegance of Renaissance drawings, and so many other teachings we ignore, since we only study past generations' arts to copy them. And with these rigorously proven principles, let us openly apply the forms that new experiences and needs impose on us by enriching them and giving them expression with the ornamental treasures that monuments from all ages and nature have to offer. In other words, let us venerate and study the past assiduously, let us seek with firm convictions what we have to do today, and let us have faith and courage to carry it out.

Maybe we shall be told that this is a new form of eclecticism: seeking the practice of all good doctrines, which as a good cannot be contradictory, is to be eclectic; assimilating like plants the air, water, and earth, the elements needed for a healthy life; believing that all generations have left us something worthy of learning and wanting to study and apply it. If it all means faltering, we declare ourselves convicted of eclecticism.

We well know this is not the road to an easy triumph for the artists who wish to follow it. Nor does the required assiduous work guarantee reaching profits today and glory tomorrow. In order to produce results, it is neither two nor three generations' work, and even when achieved, what artists have contributed today, would only be one more drop in the sea of past ideas.

Note

1   I assume that Domènech is referring to the Arsenal in Habsburg Vienna, 1848–1856, and was the first of three buildings which replaced the old city fortifications. The supervising architect-administrator was Leopold Mayr. Domènech's extensive travel through Central Europe and his impressive library of German-language architectural publications – books, periodicals, and newspapers – would have made him well aware of the buildings designated to be replaced with modern ones.

Index